MW00624493

Educating for Eternity

EDUCATING
FOR
ETERNITY

A Teacher's Companion for

Making Every
Class Catholic

BRETT SALKELD, PH.D.

Foreword by Thomas W. Carroll,
Superintendent of Schools, Archdiocese of Boston

Our Sunday Visitor
Huntington, Indiana

Our Sunday Visitor Publishing Division
Our Sunday Visitor, Inc.
200 Noll Plaza
Huntington, IN 46750
www.osv.com
1-800-348-2440

ISBN: 978-1-68192-756-5 (Inventory No. T2626)
1. EDUCATION—Philosophy—Theory & Social Aspects.
2. RELIGION—Education.
3. RELIGION—Christianity—Catholic.

eISBN: 978-1-68192-757-2
LCCN: 2022949330

Cover and Interior design: Amanda Falk
Cover and Interior art: AdobeStock

PRINTED IN THE UNITED STATES OF AMERICA

Contents

Foreword

The Catholic Church is at a critical juncture. Secularism infects almost every aspect of our culture. Religious belief, which had been gradually declining for years, is now in a freefall. In the aftermath of COVID-19, already low Mass attendance has dropped even lower. Many graduates of Catholic high schools and colleges simply do not embrace the faith of their parents and grandparents. In sum, we could be a generation away from American churches becoming museum pieces and photographic backdrops for the occasional wedding.

In the seminal book *From Christendom to Apostolic Mission*, Monsignor James Shea describes the shift from Christendom, a culture that was largely defined by Christianity, to a new Apostolic Age, in which we must go forth like the original Apostles and make our case to a broader community of nonbelievers.

As Superintendent of Schools for the Roman Catholic Archdiocese of Boston and as a Catholic convert myself, I believe

Catholic schools *properly organized* are the only way we can rebuild our Church and religious belief in America. I say "properly organized" because many Catholic schools are not presently organized for the Apostolic Age in which we find ourselves. Catholic schools have lost their evangelizing focus, and as a result, we are facing widespread disbelief, and far too many believers who are poorly catechized.

Educating for Eternity is the guidebook that should be in the hands of every Catholic educator in the nation. We need to remake our Catholic schools to be engines of evangelization. This will only happen if we hire teachers committed and equipped to evangelize and we also give them the training and tools to "make every class Catholic," as suggested by Brett Salkeld, Ph.D., in this important book.

Salkeld correctly perceives that making every class Catholic is a daunting task. To do so, teachers in Catholic schools must be willing to share their ideas with one another in an open-source way. Social media has corrupted our culture in many ways, but sharing ideas on Facebook and other social media platforms is an important way for this new movement to go viral and take hold in classroom after classroom.

Within schools themselves, a few steps are needed. First, those with responsibility for Catholic schools need to become fishers of men and women, who joyfully embrace Catholicism and the evangelizing mission of Catholic schools. Like Jesus, we need to find our apostles. Catholic schools should hire authentic witnesses to our Catholic faith. Pope St. Paul VI astutely observed: "Modern man listens more willingly to witnesses than to teachers, and if he does listen to teachers, it is because they are witnesses."

Second, Catholic schools should be brave in proclaiming the truth. Foundational beliefs — for example, the sanctity of life and that God created man and woman — must be proclaimed and not downplayed simply because they are rejected by many in the broader culture.

Third, Catholic schools should fully embrace Catholic contributions to our culture and world. These include: the Catholic intellectual tradition, which has no rival in the secular world; the many Catholic contributions to fields as diverse as art, architecture, literature, law, philosophy, science, and human rights; and the global footprint of the Church in serving the poor, dispossessed, and marginalized.

Fourth, Catholic schools should choose carefully the textbooks and educational materials they use. Most mass-market secular textbooks simply should not be used in a Catholic school. The Catholic Textbook Project has done much great work to provide suitable alternatives. But *Educating for Eternity*'s biggest contribution may be prompting a much broader, bottom-up sharing of ideas and content.

Fifth, religion in a Catholic school must not be relegated only to theology or religion classes. For all the reasons articulated in this important book, every academic subject should be reviewed anew to determine appropriate and authentic ways that Catholic contributions and a Catholic voice may be added.

As someone who converted only twenty years ago, I am not arguing for Catholic schools only for Catholic children. Evangelizing presupposes that we welcome with open arms students from different cultures and religions. Free will is central to Church teaching; so, we don't command belief. But we do have an obligation to draw children closer to God and to share the light of truth with them. The Vatican, through the Congregation for Catholic Education, beautifully expressed this balance in the document entitled *The Identity of the Catholic School for a Culture of Dialogue* (2022).

In this context, I believe that *Educating for Eternity* will become the indispensable handbook for a renewed apostolic effort to salvage our culture and Church by helping teachers and leaders find their school's Catholic voice. Because of the influence of *Educating for Eternity*, countless children will be set on the path to eternal salvation — and the Church itself may be given new life as well.

Thomas W. Carroll
Superintendent of Schools, Archdiocese of Boston

Preface
How to Use This Book

The primary purpose of this book is to equip Catholic teachers to approach every subject that they teach from a Catholic point of view and thereby to aid them in their mission of transmitting a living and vibrant Catholic faith to their students. It is written from the conviction that Catholic schools must be distinct from other schools not merely by the presence of religion class, nor even by the presence of a genuinely Catholic ethos pervading the relationships that constitute the school community (as essential as these two items most certainly are), but by the way in which a Catholic worldview informs academic instruction in every subject area.

The practice of teaching every subject from a Catholic point of view is sometimes referred to as curriculum permeation. The good people at the McGrath Center for Church Life at the University of Notre Dame call it Catholic Academic Integration, or

CAI, a term coined by the Center's Senior Learning Designer Clare Kilbane. But whatever it might be called in your context, it is an essential component of any genuinely Catholic education. And while there is no shortage of books written about Catholic education, I have not found one dedicated specially to this fundamental task. As our culture becomes more and more post-Christian, and as the basic cultural presuppositions through which we unwittingly approach any subject become correspondingly less and less Catholic, we must be ever more intentional about cultivating a consistent and coherent Catholic worldview in ourselves and in our students. Such a worldview will impact the way we approach every subject.

I wrote this book with several audiences in mind. **First,** I was writing for Catholic teachers already working in the field. Many of these teachers have been encouraged to "permeate" or "infuse" their lesson plans with their Catholic faith, but have not always been given the training to do so. For some it comes naturally, but for others it feels like an awkward imposition on top of how they were trained to teach. This book, then, is first and foremost a professional development resource for Catholic teachers. Catholic schools or school divisions that offer courses to introduce new staff into the vocation of Catholic education will find it particularly useful.

It can, of course, be read by individual teachers but is also intended as a resource for a school staff to read together, discuss, and put into practice as a team. For example, individual departments could focus on particular chapters in Part II and do presentations to the whole staff about their specific subject area, looking for cross-curricular connections with colleagues in other departments. The "Key Takeaways" provided at the end of each chapter should help lock in learning and could be used to focus group discussions. I have also provided a set of reflection/discussion questions in the introduction to Part II to help teachers apply insights from each of the chapters in Part II in their classrooms.

Second, this book can be used as a textbook in university classes, either for undergraduates studying to become Catholic teachers, or for teachers doing graduate work in Catholic education. Indeed, I first explored the content of this book — especially Part I — in a Philosophy of Catholic Education course I taught for aspiring Catholic teachers at Campion College in Regina, Saskatchewan. The reflection questions at the beginning of Part II might be used to frame assignments in such a class.

No book can do everything. This book is not a book of lesson plans (though I do offer some ideas throughout the text), nor is it a proposed curriculum. It is, rather, an introduction to the idea of Catholic Academic Integration that is designed to be of use to teachers no matter what curricula they are already responsible for teaching. While there may be certain elements that require careful discernment, and even critique, you do not need to change a whole curriculum to begin teaching it from a Catholic point of view! That said, a **third** audience for this book is those in Catholic education who *do* work in curriculum development or who produce the kinds of resources Catholic teachers use in the classroom every day. This book provides these professionals with both foundational principles and a wealth of specific ideas for such work. (I think that someone who designs classroom posters, for example, will find lots of ideas here. Actually, if you do that work, e-mail me. We should talk!)

Fourth, there are many Catholics — parents, clergy, religious, academics, writers, home educators — who are deeply interested in the question of Catholic education because of their commitment to passing on the Faith to our children and their recognition of the essential role of education in the mission of the Church. This group, too, will find in these pages a vision for Catholic education that is both attentive to principles and full of practical implications.

Fifth, and finally, because the classroom is a key place of encounter between the Church and the broader culture, a book that is written to empower teachers to be fully and faithfully Catholic through the lens of their subject areas will be of interest to any Catholic who want to think about how to respond to the challenges that contemporary culture puts to the Church. The things we study in science or health or social studies are the same kinds of things that the Church must be thinking about critically and creatively in order to develop and present a credible witness to the world. It is my hope that anyone who reads this book, whether or not they are employed in the noble work of Catholic education, will come away with a clearer vision of how their Catholic faith informs how they approach many of the most important questions facing our Church and our world.

This book is divided into two parts. Part I is dedicated to thinking through several key elements of what makes a Catholic education Catholic. Catholic Academic Integration is not merely about adding some Catholic content to our classes where possible. It starts with thinking about the task of education in general from a Catholic perspective, and not simply taking the assumptions of the broader culture for granted.

Part II begins with an introduction to the idea that Catholicism shapes our approach to each subject area. The rest of Part II is an exploration of eight key subject areas — Literature and Language Arts, History, Math, Science, Civics and Social Studies, Health, Sports and Physical Education, and Art — from a Catholic point of view. The introduction to this part should be read first, but the subject-specific chapters can, despite occasional references to previous chapters, be read in any order. The one partial exception here is that the Art chapter will be read more profitably if the reader is familiar with the Literature and Language Arts chapter.

Reading a book can be a great form of professional development. But the impact of such reading will be amplified if the reader makes a commitment to practices that will support her learning and has the support of a community of other practitioners. To that end, I want to invite you to join the Making Every Class Catholic group on Facebook. There you can find additional resources and share ideas with other teachers. There will be regular posts tagged with #MakingEveryClassCatholic as well as subject-specific tags such as #MakingScienceClassCatholic or #MakingHistoryClassCatholic. You can search these tags on Facebook or Twitter for a growing library of resources to help you think about your subject area from a Catholic point of view.

Part I
What Are People For?

You have made us for yourself, O Lord, and our hearts are restless until they rest in you.

SAINT AUGUSTINE

"What are people for?" There's a good chance you've never been asked this question so directly. But whether you have or not, take a minute to think about your own answer to it. If you're really keen, or you're reading this for class and your prof asked you to, try writing a paragraph or two explaining your answer before reading the rest of this chapter. I'll be here when you get back.

Now, what is this question doing at the beginning of a book about Catholic education? Education is never neutral! It is always oriented toward a goal or set of goals. Some people think education is mainly about getting skills to compete in the job market. Others think it is primarily about raising social consciousness. Others that a good education is to teach people how to think critically.

Some people have thought explicitly and intentionally about what an education is for, and others have simply assumed that an education is basically a good thing that everyone should have without pursuing the question of its goals very deeply. That last option should not be available to teachers, least of all Catholic teachers.

Every education *presumes an anthropology.* That is to say, every education is directed, intentionally or not, by underlying attitudes about the human person. What makes people happy? Is happiness even a worthwhile goal? What goods should people pursue? Are there things people should avoid? What makes for a good life? Are these questions even answerable for people in general? Or must every person figure out on his or her own how best to live? What are people anyway? And what are they for?

An education that presumes that people are for the economy (that we are, at root, *homo economicus*) will have certain features and emphases. An education that presumes that people are for the state (that we are, first and foremost, *citizens*) will have slightly different features and emphases. I say "slightly" because very often the interests of the economy and the interests of the state overlap. Good citizens, as we learned immediately after 9/11, are people who shop!

Allow me to be bold for a moment. There is a word the Bible uses to describe these presumptions: *idolatry.* Idolatry does not simply mean the worship of evil or evil things. In fact, that type of idolatry is quite rare. What is much more common is the worship of (literally, the granting of too much *worth* to) things that are good in themselves. That is to say, idolatry happens most easily when we pursue a lower good at the expense of a higher one. Jobs are good. But when we pursue them at the expense of our relationships with our families, we do great damage. Health is a great good, but if we pursue it as the highest good, we set ourselves up for guaranteed disappointment. We all get sick, and we all die.

According to the Christian tradition, the best, indeed the only, way to make sure that all the competing goods that we try to balance in this life are in order is to worship God alone. All earthly goods — and they are genuinely good — take on their proper place and proportion when none of them is treated as ultimate.

There is a very troubling verse in the Gospel of Luke where Jesus says, "Whoever comes to me and does not hate father and mother, wife and children, brothers and sisters, yes, and even life itself, cannot be my disciple" (14:26). To understand this verse, we need to recognize that Jesus is not saying we must actually hate our families. Remember, he also said, in John 13:34, "I give you a new commandment, that you love one another. Just as I have loved you, you also should love one another." That is, you must love one another to the point of giving up your lives for each other. What Jesus is saying in Luke 14 is that anyone who would let family relationships, opinions, squabbles, obligations, etc., come before Christian discipleship is doing it wrong. When we commit our life to Christian discipleship, we will sometimes be rejected, even by our own families. And even then, we should be willing to suffer on behalf of those who reject us. This is the kind of love Jesus shows us on the cross.

MADE FOR GOD

*It was a fundamental principle of the Gradgrind philoso-
phy that everything was to be paid for. Nobody was ever on
any account to give anybody anything, or render anybody
help without purchase. Gratitude was to be abolished, and
the virtues springing from it were not to be. Every inch of
the existence of mankind, from birth to death, was to be
a bargain across a counter. And if we didn't get to Heaven
that way, it was not a politico-economical place, and we
had no business there.*

CHARLES DICKENS, HARD TIMES

To put God first is not to deny the goodness of the created order,
of families and jobs and healthy bodies, of festivity and intimacy.
It is to prioritize them rightly so that we are able to sacrifice the
lower goods for the sake of the higher ones. The anthropology,
the vision of the human person, at the heart of Catholic education, then, is the presumption that we are not made for the economy or the state; we are not made for pleasure or for health; we
are not even ultimately made for family: We are made for God.

Now it is very tempting for contemporary western people,
even practicing Catholics, to recoil slightly at this. If people want
to say that God is their first priority, they can feel free to do so in
their own homes, and even in their places of worship on Sunday.
But can we really import this into schools that are, after all, part
of the apparatus of the state? Even private schools that receive no
public funding are a part of this apparatus at least to the degree
that they exempt students from having to attend other schools.
No matter *where* you get your formal education, some formal
education *is* mandated by the state.

It is very easy for an education system to worship at the altar of the economy and of the state — that is, to make jobs and citizenship the highest goals of education — because these are understood to be common goals that we share with all our neighbors, whether or not they share our religious convictions. And make no mistake, Catholics *are* called to work with all people of good will for the common good of our communities, whether local, national, or international.

But we cannot, therefore, accept the idea that education is primarily about forming people for the economy and for citizenship. Claims about ultimate goods cannot be relegated to the private sphere. While it is often asserted that this is done in order to respect the freedom of the religious (or nonreligious) convictions of all, in reality it is just the opposite. Relegating religious belief to the private sphere is a clear statement that what humanity has always considered to be the most important questions are not, in fact, very important at all. When we banish the big questions from education, we do not simply reserve them for people's private judgment in conscience; we teach by our actions that they are less important than the "real work" we do in schools.

So, Catholic schools and a Catholic education have to be built upon the premise that people are for God. And while education should certainly prepare students for the job market and responsible citizenship, these are subsidiary goals that must never blind us to the highest goal. We must not convey the impression (which is very easy to convey in our culture) that the economy and the state are the highest goods for which we sacrifice all other goods.

THERE IS NO NEUTRAL

But what does the notion that we are made for God mean in practical terms? And how does that change what happens in the classroom?

This book is an attempt to answer just that question. The important thing to recognize here is that our approach to any subject will be determined, whether or not we are aware of it, by our basic worldview and the goals we believe an education should pursue. So, the first thing is to learn to recognize our unspoken and even unacknowledged assumptions (part of what is sometimes called the "hidden curriculum") and how those impact the way we understand and present the content we are responsible for. For example, do we imagine that math class is simply about learning marketable skills so that we can become capable and productive engineers and accountants? Or do we also understand math as an exploration of the beauty and order of creation that can teach us something about the Creator? Two plus two equals four in either classroom, but what two plus two equaling four *means* for human life and human flourishing is radically different in these two approaches.

It is easy to imagine that the content we present, especially in something like math, is essentially "neutral." And so, to infuse a Catholic worldview into our teaching can seem like a kind of corruption of the pure subject matter, maybe even a kind of brainwashing. But the fact is that even something as seemingly neutral as math will be taught from some point of view or other. What we think about the goals of the human person, and therefore the goals of education, will orient our approach to every subject. If people are made for God, then math class will be, first and foremost, an exploration of God's beautiful and orderly creation. If people are made for the economy, then math class will be primarily a place to acquire marketable skills.

Remarkably, students in a math class that is first and foremost an exploration of God's creation will be at no disadvantage for developing marketable skills. But a math class that prioritizes the marketable outcomes may indeed undercut its own aims. The best math teachers, even if they are not explicitly religious, convey a deep sense of wonder that is infectious. They fire their students' imaginations so that math becomes exciting. This not only leads to more and better professionals in mathematical fields, but to a greater sense of purpose and satisfaction for those professionals, who understand themselves as participating in a beautiful creation and not simply as crunching numbers to pay the bills. It leads, that is, to a more fully human life.

If this is true of math class, it is true of every class. And so, after learning to recognize that teaching our subject matter from a neutral point of view is impossible and to identify the underlying ideas and priorities that inform our teaching, our next step, as Catholic teachers, is to become more and more fluent in the Catholic worldview, particularly as that relates to our own areas of teaching specialization. A Catholic history teacher should not only develop expertise in history, but in a Catholic understanding of history. The same goes for every other subject. There is no neutral, and if we do not teach from a Catholic point of view, we will teach from some other point of view. And brainwashing is, in fact, a much greater danger if we imagine ourselves to be teaching from a neutral place that does not actually exist than if we are open and honest about our own commitments.

SEEK YE FIRST

But strive first for the kingdom of God and his righteousness, and all these things will be given to you as well.

MATTHEW 6:33

There are lots of reasons why even Catholics might be tempted to emphasize the temporal goals of education. No one denies that things like a good job and responsible citizenship are worthy goals. A Catholic education is interested in such matters. But if the ultimate goal of the human person is to be happy forever with God, these goals need to be subordinated to the higher goal of cultivating our students' relationship with God. Still, one might ask, is that really what education is about? Many contemporary people think that religion is a private matter and education is a public one. While it is tricky for a Catholic teacher to think this explicitly, it is easy to be unwittingly influenced by those who do. Sometimes Catholic educators are tempted to believe we need to prove ourselves by being better at achieving temporal goals than other schools. More than that, some people think that a focus on eternal things is a distraction from the real business of life. It is not uncommon to hear the suggestion that the promise of heaven keeps believers from improving the world we live in — that we are too heavenly minded to be any earthly good.

But a Catholic education is supposed to prepare people for eternal life and for the fullness of life in the here and now. Can it do both? And how do these two things fit together?

While many people have accused Christianity of forsaking the task of making this world better by promising people paradise after death, the simple fact is that countless Christians throughout history have labored to make the world a better place. Think of people like Mother Teresa, or Martin Luther King Jr., or William Wilberforce, who spearheaded the abolition of slavery in Britain and the British colonies, or the literally thousands of religious sisters who have given their lives to humanity serving in hospitals and schools. Not to mention the millions upon millions of loving parents, helpful neighbors, and other everyday saints inspired by the Gospel. Were these people content to leave the world as they found it because heaven is all that really matters? Obviously not! But why not?

Let me suggest two reasons. The first is that people like

Mother Teresa and Martin Luther King Jr. and the whole Christian tradition with them do not see a radical divide between being with God forever in heaven and building God's kingdom here on earth. These are not two different goals, but two parts of the same goal. God does not plan to destroy creation, but to redeem the whole of it. Christian salvation is not escaping from a wrecked ship that is going down in any case. Rather, it is the leading edge of the redemption of the entire cosmos, including — as the image of the New Jerusalem (i.e., a city) in the Book of Revelation (chapter 21) symbolizes — human social structures. Working for the redemption of the world is already implied in the Christian notion of salvation. This does not mean rescuing some other lucky individuals from the shipwreck; it means changing the world. Those who are most gripped by a love of God and a desire to be with him forever are the most, not the least, motivated to make a difference here on earth.

Of course, there are many other people who want to make a difference on earth too. If this is motivated by a genuine love for humanity, a Catholic is inclined to believe that such people genuinely love God as well, even if they don't know that is what they are doing. Jesus is pretty clear in Matthew 25:31–46 that anyone serving those most in need is really serving him, whether they know it or not. Nevertheless, there are those who, in their zeal for changing the world, lose sight of actual humanity. Indeed, literally millions of people have been sacrificed at the altar of changing the world. This is one way of understanding the stunning human violence of the twentieth century. The logic is essentially the same whether we are considering the Nazi death camps, the Soviet gulags, or the millions of children aborted in their mothers' wombs. In each case, an ideological agenda sought to change the world and was willing to countenance human slaughter on an industrial scale to achieve it. If a person believes that his cause is absolutely critical, and that the success of that cause is tenuous, he can justify almost any means to attain it. And people have. This is the truth behind the adage that those who try to create heaven on earth end up creating hell instead. Idols always demand sacrifice.

Which brings us to the second reason why a desire for God and a hope for heaven have made Christians able to change the world for the better. Because not everything depends on our success! If a person believes that God is the most powerful actor in history, that God has a plan for humanity, and that God will finally achieve that plan, that person can work through the worst setbacks without succumbing to despair. Mother Teresa could watch thousands suffer and die and still get up every morning to go and care for more. Martin Luther King Jr. and his followers could get beaten up in the streets and then find a church in which to praise God for their beatings. Because they knew they were working on God's side of history, they never had to resort to the kinds of tactics that a person can easily come to think are necessary if everything depends on him, here and now.

Anyone who thinks that humans can, with the right political program, create a utopia has not paid sufficient attention to history. More than that, he has not even really taken an honest look into his own heart. It is hard enough to live peacefully in a house full of people we sincerely love, people for whom we might well be willing to offer our lives. The deepest problem is not that our political system is inadequate — however true that may be — but that we are sinners.

Fortunately for us, God knew our weaknesses full well when he sent his Son to do for us what we could never do for ourselves: to sacrifice himself (idols never do that!) not just for those closest to him, but for the very people lynching him on the cross. And what God began on that cross, he continues to work out in history. We are called to accompany him, to serve him by serving one another, to get a little better at offering our lives even for our enemies. But we are not called to save the world. It's not our job. And it is the freedom that comes from not having to save the world that has allowed Christians throughout history to serve without counting the cost or calculating the outcome, without despairing and resorting to measures that, while they aim to eliminate evil, only perpetuate it. We are free to participate in God's work because God's success does not ultimately depend on ours.

A Catholic education is an education in just this type of freedom. It equips students to change the world, not by engaging in the power games of this world, but by becoming who they are called to be in Christ. It is not just about learning facts or marketable skills. It is, first and foremost, about learning what matters, what is valuable, what is good, and becoming the kind of person who can act accordingly more and more often. A person who knows all kinds of things but has no idea how to integrate that knowledge into a life well lived is not educated. An educated person has a framework within which to put his knowledge to work, to make sense of the world, to set priorities, and to make decisions. A Catholic education prepares people for success in the world, though not always in the ways the world measures success. But more than that, an authentic Catholic education forms people who can change the world, not in spite of their desire for God and their hope for heaven, but because of it.

KEY TAKEAWAYS

An education is never neutral. It is always structured by our understanding of what makes for human flourishing, even if we have not thought about this explicitly.

Humans are made for God, and putting God first allows us to rightly prioritize all the other competing goods in our lives.

Every subject is taught from some point of view or other. There is no neutral. A fully integrated Catholic worldview will impact how every subject matter is approached.

Pursuing God with our whole hearts is the best preparation for making a difference in the world.

Chapter 1
Joy, Virtue, and Holiness

What kind of knowledge do we need to impart to our students so that they can be successful in a changing world? What skills will they need to make it in the twenty-first century? Perhaps you've been part of discussions or read books and articles concerned with precisely these questions.

When I was young, we were often told that computer programming was an essential skill in the workplace of the future. As it turned out, only a small number of people really needed specialized skills in computer programming, and the vast majority of us use computers every day without ever having officially studied much more than some basic word processing.

But it is not just that the people who predicted we would all become computer programmers guessed the wrong skill. Their first mistake was thinking that education was primarily about knowledge and skills in the first place. They presumed that an education is successful if people come out the end of it *knowing* the important things or perhaps simply *able to do* the important things. But knowledge and skills aren't the most important things for a good life. Think about it. What are the biggest obstacles to you living a better life?

If you're like most people, your life would be better if you could do things like manage your time well; make priorities and follow through on them; understand your own emotions and express them appropriately; say what you mean and mean what you say; stand up for yourself and others effectively and charitably; let go of a grudge; ask for and offer forgiveness; presume well of others; set healthy boundaries around difficult relationships; or eat, drink, sleep, exercise, work, watch Netflix, or scroll social media as much or as little as you discern is good for you and not as much or as little as you feel like at the time. Most of us would improve our lives significantly if we could simply believe in the goodness God intended when he created us. In other words, you would live better and be a happier person if you had virtues like patience, humility, courage, honesty, chastity, prudence, self-control, faith, hope, and love.

If the ultimate goal of a Catholic education is to get us to heaven, the primary this-worldly goal of a Catholic education is not knowledge or skills, as valuable as those are, but character. A Catholic education seeks to form a student into someone who can live well — because becoming who God calls us to be is where eternity touches this world right now. A person of character, a person with the kinds of virtues listed above, is both free and joyful. And a free and joyful person can live a good life in almost any occupation.

THE GOOD LIFE

The only real sadness, the only real failure, the only
great tragedy in life, is not to become a saint.

LÉON BLOY, THE WOMAN WHO WAS POOR

Our culture often misunderstands how morality works. We tend
to think of morality as a series of restrictions on our freedom, a
list of things we can't do because they are bad. Sometimes they
are obviously bad because they harm us and others, and sometimes they seem to have been just arbitrarily labeled "bad" by
some authority figure or outdated tradition. But that is not really morality. Rather, morality is about becoming more and more
free to live a good life.

Consider your own experience. Where do you experience
freedom? And where do you experience unfreedom? If you
are someone who struggles with self-control, but not so much
with humility, you feel (and actually are!) quite free when those
around you are getting accolades while your contributions go
unnoticed or unmentioned, but you do not feel very free at all
when you keep picking up your smartphone during your kid's
soccer game even though you know you shouldn't.

And, if we'll admit it, most of us have more serious problems
than our smartphone addictions. In his letter to the Romans,
Saint Paul labeled our experience of unfreedom in an unforget-
table way: "For I delight in the law of God in my inmost self, but I
see in my members another law at war with the law of my mind,
making me captive to the law of sin that dwells in my members.
Wretched man that I am! Who will rescue me from this body of
death?" (7:22–24). Who among us has not felt this disconnect
within ourselves at some point or another?

Of course, none of us wants to sign up for a morality that

just takes away the things we like to do or makes us feel guilty for them. But who among us does not wish to be more patient, more humble, more self-controlled? When we actually are patient or humble or self-controlled, we are happy! And the better we get at those virtues, the happier they make us.

We have all experienced the strange mixture of happiness and regret that is the first step toward virtue. Like when you hold your tongue after an infuriating comment and think up a really biting rebuttal to yourself in the car on the way home. For a moment you think, "I should have told that so-and-so what's what," but then you think, "Actually, it's probably for the best that I didn't. In fact, I'm not even sure *how* I didn't, but I'm glad I didn't."

The person who can hold her tongue even when sorely tempted is at the beginning of virtue. But growth in virtue does not consist in facing down ever more grievous temptations, though that may well happen. Rather it consists in becoming less and less tempted by the things that have troubled you in the past. The person who holds her tongue once is more likely to hold it again the next time she is tempted. And the person who holds her tongue many times forms such a habit that what used to be a great temptation no longer troubles her. We are glad when we hold our tongues in moments of trial, but we live more freely and joyfully when things that used to infuriate us and sorely tempt us no longer even show up on our radars. *That* is the relationship between growth in virtue and freedom — and joy!

STEP BY STEP

But we are often afraid to take the first step because we imagine that the journey itself is so difficult that any progress we make at these early stages will not amount to anything. In many ways, though, the first step is the hardest one because each step afterwards is able to build on that first small victory. This is why growth in virtue relies not so much on an act of superhuman willpower — in fact, anyone who has tried that strategy knows just how unlikely it is to work — but on God's grace. Now, Catholics will insist that we need to engage our freedom to cooperate with God's grace. Grace is not magic. But God is still the one supplying the real power behind any progress we make.

Consider this: Just as we saw in the introduction to Part I that Christians are free to change the world precisely because its salvation does not ultimately depend on us, Christians are free to try and fail, and try and fail, and try and fail again in the moral life because our moral progress does not ultimately depend on us. We believe in and love a God who does not hold our failures against us, but, like a parent teaching a child to walk, encourages us to stand up each time we fall and to try again. And every time we try again, we are a little closer to the goal by the simple fact of having not given up. If we keep accepting God's invitations to try again, we will find, seemingly miraculously, that progress happens almost in spite of ourselves.

To do only the little that is available to you in the moment is to make more available in the next moment. God does not ask for more than that. In fact, God's grace is working with you to make more available to you. Every time you cooperate with grace, you open yourself more and more to its influence. The paradox is that, as hard as growth in virtue is, in some ways, when it is actually achieved, it can feel almost too easy. One day you notice something that would have once been a grave temptation for you — a donut, an inconsiderate driver, a mirror, a spouse who misreads your intentions, a great sale for something you don't really need, time alone with an internet connection, a gossipy conversation, illness, an argument on social media — is just not a thing for you anymore. Growth in virtue isn't so much about climbing bigger and bigger mountains with ever more effort, but about becoming capable of taking bigger and bigger steps so that big things start to seem smaller. Or maybe it is about learning how small some of the things were all along.

HOLINESS

All of this is, by the way, just another way of talking about holiness. Many of us are nervous about overly pious-sounding language. We don't want to be perceived as "holier-than-thou." Indeed, some of us might have been a bit taken aback by the starkness of the quote from Léon Bloy earlier in this chapter. Somewhere along the line, we might even have been given the impression that holiness is for saints, not ordinary folk like us. And we might be quite comfortable in the notion that holiness is not for us. But "I'm no saint" is more often employed as a feeble excuse than as a simple statement of fact. The Church is clear, and this was a key theme of the Second Vatican Council, that all Christians are called to holiness. The saints were not born that way. There is not some pre-existing group of people called "saints" that some people just happen to belong to. Saints are ordinary folks like us who learned (some more quickly than others) to pursue God with their whole hearts. It is said that when St. Thomas Aquinas was asked, "How can one become a saint?" he answered, "Will it." The prerequisite for sainthood is not the genetics for holiness, but the desire for holiness.

Some of us might not even know if we want holiness or not. We worry, perhaps, that it will mean giving up on things we think we love or need, that the demands of holiness are too great, that we are incapable or unworthy. But here's the thing: Saint You is exactly the person you would choose to be if you could. If it were as simple as choosing it, no one would choose to be less patient rather than more, to have less self-control rather than more, to be less humble or honest or courageous rather than more. If we actually understood that chastity is not just abstinence but the freedom and self-possession to give ourselves — because we are actually in possession of ourselves — to our spouse or religious community as we are called, we'd even choose to be more chaste. Indeed, we've all met people whose lives would be better, happier, and freer if they had more of the virtue of chastity; most of us *are* those people. If we really understood what holiness is and believed that it is possible, we would all want to be saints.

DESIRING GOD

But store up for yourselves treasures in heaven … for where you treasure is, there your heart will be also.

MATTHEW 6:20–21

Modern people tend to imagine that what we *think* is the most fundamental thing about who we are. This attitude has a deep impact on education, because it means that the most important thing is getting people to think the right things. Want to change the world? Change people's wrong ideas about the world! Many of us who have bought into this find ourselves endlessly frustrated by the seeming irrationality of those with whom we disagree. Can't they just *see*?! Worse than that, if we are honest, we know that even *we* don't act according to what *we think* best.

The advertising industry knows something that the rest of us usually miss. They know what Thomas Aquinas knew when he said that the way to become a saint was to will it. They know what Saint Augustine knew when he said, "My weight is my love. Wherever I am carried, my love is carrying me." They know that *what we know* is far less determinative for our decisions than what we want, what we desire, *what we love.*

Have you ever seen old advertisements for automobiles or cleaning products that discuss, in detailed paragraphs, the attributes of the product with disarming honesty? Don't they seem quaint? These ads can even induce a longing in us for a time when we did not feel constantly manipulated by media. Here was an honest person with a good product who would sell it to you if it suited your budget and your needs. Isn't that how capitalism was supposed to work? Now we don't even expect car ads to give us any useful information about cars. We expect them to stoke our desire.

A Catholic education should know what the advertising industry knows, namely, that our desires have more weight than our thoughts. And it should know this not in order to manipulate us like the ad agencies, but to free us from such manipulation. If we are attentive to forming our own desires — or better, letting God form our desires — we are far less susceptible to having them formed for us without our knowledge or consent. This shows up all over our tradition, in the wisdom of the saints, in the reflections of our theologians, even on the lips of Jesus himself: "Store up for yourselves treasure in heaven ... for where you treasure is, there your heart will be also" (Mt 6:21). A Catholic education should not just teach Catholic morality, though it should certainly do that, but it must stoke the desire for the good. It should make the good seem beautiful, desirable, and possible.

MADE FOR GREATNESS

The world offers you comfort. But you were not made for comfort. You were made for greatness.

ATTRIBUTED TO POPE BENEDICT XVI

One of the great sadnesses of contemporary culture is the degree to which irony, even cynicism, has become our default approach to goodness. Young children earnestly desire to be good, and when they turn from that, it is usually pretty easy to see an unmet need, say, for attention, that is driving that turn. Such earnestness can be almost heartbreaking. And surely one of the saddest things we can watch is the child, earnest for good, turning slowly into the jaded teen. We might almost think this transformation is inevitable, a normal part of human development. It's not.

People become jaded or hide behind irony because it feels safe and because they do not have anything real to hope for. A Catholic education should fill a child with hope that her life has meaning, that she is called by God to some great work, that she is capable (with God's grace) of being, actually, good.

Why are the books of the *The Lord of the Rings* trilogy some of the most popular books of all time? Even among millions of nonbelievers? Because they speak to a longing deep in the human heart that even seemingly insignificant people can be part of great adventures that matter. They fan the flames of hope for meaning and purpose in our hearts. They make us desire the good. They make us desire it so deeply that we would be willing to sacrifice all manner of comfort and security to have a role in a story that mattered that much.

But J. R. R. Tolkien, a devout Catholic, could only write *The Lord of the Rings* because he already believed that we really do have such a role in such a story. To the Catholic imagination, life is always an adventure, a quest, a battle. There is always the unaccountable and quiet power of the good pitted against the terrifying but ultimately self-defeating power of evil. There is always something real at stake, something worth living and worth dying for.

FOSTERING HOPE

How does a Catholic education foster and focus this universal desire to matter? How can it encourage students to develop an attitude that will sacrifice comfort for meaning, for purpose, for greatness?

In many ways. One way is through our engagement with the curriculum. This is the topic of Part II of this book. So let just a couple of examples suffice to make the point here. If we teach science in a way that imagines that the universe is a grand accident and that individual human persons are only a series of tiny coincidences inside such an accident, we communicate something very different than if we teach that creation was intended by God and that each of us was created with a purpose. This does not change the mechanics of the Big Bang one whit, but it completely changes the *meaning* of the Big Bang. And this is not just a matter of personal preference, as if it only changes the meaning of the Big Bang *for us* because *we* choose to believe that. No, if God created us with a purpose, then the meaning of the Big Bang *really is* different than if we are just a cosmic coincidence.

Or, if we teach a cynical piece of contemporary literature, we communicate something very different if we imagine such literature as savvy and self-aware than if we dig deeper and realize that cynicism, however brilliant, is often a cover for hopelessness. And, of course, we teach something simply by the choice of a cynical piece of literature over a noble and beautiful piece. These kinds of decisions in presenting the material in the curriculum — decisions that we are often not even aware of making — shape the desires and the hopes of our students.

INSPIRING OUR STUDENTS

What else can direct our desires well? Role models. This, of course, means teachers, as every teacher knows. But have we thought about what being a role model means from a Catholic point of view? A role model is not just someone who follows the rules or keeps her dirty laundry private. A role model's life makes the young *desire the good*.

Do we live in a way that inspires? And, if not, is it because we have stopped believing in the possibility of the good ourselves? None of us is going to be perfect at this, but if you want to be an inspiration to your students, *start by believing good things about them.* If this is a struggle sometimes, try this: Pray that the Holy Spirit would show you the good in each of your students. Pray for them by name. Pray for the hardest cases most of all. There is little in this world that can turn a kid around like having someone believe something good about them. And our Catholic faith tells us that God created every person with a specific good in mind. It might be hard to see, but it is never absent.

But the weight isn't all on teachers, thank God. Our Catholic Faith is full of role models. Most of our schools are named for them. The stories of the saints are a rich resource for teachers. There are saints who have struggled with almost every issue under the sun. The saints are old and young, women and men, rich and poor, married and celibate, learned and simple, healthy and sick. And many saints got their start by reading lives of the saints! Why? Because those lives shaped the desires of their readers.

Almost everything we do shapes our desires. We are desiring creatures, and our desires are very malleable. We find them shifting all the time based on the slightest provocations. And so, we could ask ourselves about how each facet of school (and home and parish) life shapes desire. Education doesn't just happen in class; it happens everywhere, all the time, for good or ill. But let us conclude with one thing we do in Catholic schools that is, whether we've ever noticed it or not, explicitly about directing desire.

WORSHIP

There is no such thing as not worshipping. Everybody worships. The only choice we get is what to worship.

DAVID FOSTER WALLACE

Worship is an awkward concept for modern people. We suspect it means something like stroking the divine ego. Like God is temperamental and needs constant coddling and attention. And since worship makes us nervous, we treat religious services largely as classrooms. After all, we imagine that what we think is the key question. We are OK with learning about God. But worshipping?

Christianity, though, has always been clear that God does not *need* our worship. God is God. God doesn't *need* anything. Rather, it is we that need to worship God. We do not cower before an angry god that demands our worship to gratify his ego; we are grateful that we are able to worship the real God "in spirit and in truth" (Jn 4:24).

Why do we need to worship God? For at least two reasons. First of all, we are not God; we do not exist in our own right and by our own power. We only exist because God created us to share his eternal joy out of his own immeasurable goodness. A "thank you" would seem in order. And not because God is cranky without one, but because we are less able to live well if we do not recognize and even celebrate the truth of our own situation. We are made by God, for God. Worship is about acknowledging reality.

Second, we need to worship God because we are going to worship something. There's no "neutrality" possible here either! We are worshipping creatures. We grant *worth*. We will have some set of values and priorities, whether conscious and intentional or not, that shapes our decisions. There is no way around it. And these are not just the things we know and think but, at a more fundamental level, the things we desire and love. Our desires have been misshapen by our encounters with the world. We have been lied to about what is good, what is possible, what will make us happy. We hurt ourselves and others when we pursue these twisted desires. As we saw in the introduction, this is the meaning of idolatry. And it makes us miserable. Worship is where we let God reshape and heal our desires.

In Christian worship, and especially at Mass, we are retold the story of the God who loves us, who sacrificed for us, who invites us to join ourselves to his sacrifice, who desires for us to participate in the salvation of the world. And we are not only told the story, but we are literally placed at its very center when Christ's sacrifice is sacramentally re-presented and we receive his Body and Blood in the Eucharist. It is here that we become who we are called to be precisely by forgetting ourselves for a moment, where we learn to desire the good, even if it is costly, where we learn to see ourselves and our world from God's point of view.

Not that each of us has this subjective experience at every Mass. Far from it. But this is what the Mass is meant to do, what it does do at an objective level — whether we are paying attention or not, whether it is celebrated well or not — and what we can learn to look for in it. And learning to recognize this won't hurt our efforts if we end up being asked to organize a school Mass. We teach something that even a very good religion class will find it tough to counter if we treat a school Mass primarily as a logistical nightmare and don't appear to give much thought to what the Mass *is*.

FORMATION, NOT INFORMATION

An education is, in the end, far more about formation than information. Our job as Catholic educators is to form students, inside and outside of class, into people who know that they are made for greatness and understand what true greatness is; people who believe in the possibility of a good life and are cultivating the virtues needed to live it; people who are willing and able, even eager, to sacrifice lower goods for higher ones.

And so, when we consider the success of an education, we need to look beyond the measurable things like income, fame, or status. A Catholic education has succeeded in the patient and gentle parent, the faithful spouse, the generous neighbor, the just employer, the honest politician, the humble public figure, or the person who can be free in difficult relationships because they know their own value and dignity. A Catholic education has failed in the case of the person with all the trappings of worldly success whose inner life is a desert, whose relationships are superficial or exploitative, and who, in the final analysis, is neither free nor happy. A person of great knowledge and skill can be a danger to herself and those around her if she lacks virtue. But the person of virtue can make a good life for herself and those around her whether she makes six figures or the minimum wage.

KEY TAKEAWAYS

The most important goals of an education are not knowledge and skills but character and virtue.

Morality is not primarily about following rules, but about growing in the virtues that make us freer, happier people.

A Catholic education should strive to make being good seem both desirable and possible.

Chapter 2
Truth and Freedom

If a Catholic education is, as we argued in the last chapter, an education for freedom, we need to consider the relationship between freedom and truth. We live in a time when the very idea of truth is often held in suspicion. And the imagined connection between truth and freedom is often the opposite of the one Jesus taught in John's Gospel; we are trained to suspect that anyone making a truth claim is actually trying to impinge upon our freedom.

In public discourse today, a truth claim can be dismissed not by demonstrating that it is false, but by suggesting that it leads to consequences that are uncomfortable, undesirable, or even unfashionable. The refusal of those on either end of the political spectrum to engage with the truth claims of those on the other side, instead turning every issue into a debate about hidden motives or questions of character, is symptomatic of the basic problem. We are ofte tempted to despair of ever knowing the truth about certain questions because all we can perceive are the overwhelming biases of the sources.

Jesus said in the Gospel of John, "You will know the truth, and the truth will make you free" (Jn 8:32). But does the truth actually set us free? Or do we need to put "truth" in scare quotes because, even if there is such a thing as truth, none of us can ever have any real access to it?

MODERNISM

To understand how we got here, let us start with what philosophers call "modernism." This does not just mean contemporary (i.e., "modern") thought. Modernism, as a philosophical and cultural movement, is a couple of centuries old. It imagined that the answers to literally everything were now within our reach and proposed a narrative of human progress built on those hypothetical answers. Things as complex as history would be understood as if they were much more straightforward things like physics (at least, as straightforward as physics was imagined to be after Newton and before Einstein). It was a very optimistic movement, imagining heaven on earth was within our grasp.

The stunning success of the natural sciences had raised hopes that everything could be known as objectively and purely as the laws of nature. (Today, of course, even the natural sciences are aware of things like "observer bias" and no longer pretend to the kind of objectivity that was imagined by modernism.) Perfect knowledge in fields such as psychology and sociology would mean that we could design perfect societies as easily as a kid with a chemistry set could create a given reaction in a beaker. We needed only to learn the right formulas and then we could apply them. There was great optimism for *technical* solutions to all of humanity's problems. It was only a matter of time, or so it was thought.

The Church was highly suspicious of this movement from the start. Certainly, the Church was nervous about certain conclusions that some modernist thinkers were drawing, but the root was much deeper than that. Modernism as a narrative ignored human freedom and, therefore, the possibility of good and evil in each human person. The Church knew that there never could be a purely technical set of solutions to humanity's problems because humans are free and need to be engaged with reference to that freedom. Modernism's imagined utopia was supposed to be able to bypass human freedom and design a world so perfect that people wouldn't have to be good. The Church insisted that this was naïve and dangerous. Those who think they can make a perfect world don't just bypass human freedom; they coerce and repress it.

Though its claims have been largely refuted by history, modernism as an idea is not dead. There are still many people who believe in technical solutions to humanity's problems without reference to human freedom. Indeed, all but the most cynical among us are tempted to this idea in small ways every time we hear of a wonderful new technology. If we could manage to create nano-robots that instantaneously detect and destroy cancer cells in the human body, that would be wonderful. But it would not address the root cause of human suffering. No technology can.

There are even people today who think that a kind of perfect knowledge of all of reality is possible, generally in line with an idealized image of how the natural sciences work. Of course, for this to be true, what humans have usually meant by "all of reality" needs to be drastically pruned back. In this worldview, questions of meaning and purpose — questions of truth beyond what the natural sciences can say — become non-questions. If a given element of reality can't be reduced to a scientific question, the very idea that there is anything real that can be said about it is seen as an illusion. Everything but science becomes nothing more than a matter of personal preference. The so-called New Atheists, with their optimism about technical solutions and their breezy dismissal of nonscientific questions, are perhaps the most obvious expression of modernism today, though their influence has waned dramatically since their heyday a decade ago.

POSTMODERNISM

The history of the twentieth century shattered the grand narrative of modernism. The concentration camps and the gulags and the mass bombings of civilian populations made it very difficult to sustain the worldview that human progress was inevitable and that purely technical solutions were available to humanity's problems. If such carnage is what the most technologically advanced nations and people in the history of the world managed to achieve, the connection between technological progress and human flourishing needed serious questioning. Indeed, though many people unthinkingly follow modernism on this or that question today, a thoroughgoing optimistic modernist, of the sort common in the nineteenth century, is tough to find. We are more and more aware that technology is ambiguous, that it can be used for good or ill, and that it almost always has unintended consequences.

In the wake of the calamities of the twentieth century, postmodernism emerged on the scene as a critique of modernism. It announced the end, not simply of modernism, but of all such grand narratives. Truth, it recognized, was much more complicated than modernism thought it was. It was not objectively accessible in the abstract without reference to actual, subjective human knowers. As far as this went, the Church could only agree heartily. Indeed, the Church had been saying as much for centuries, as we will explore in the next chapter. But postmodernism didn't stop there. For many postmodern thinkers, the fact that truth was more complex than modernism imagined meant either that truth was simply not accessible to humans at all or, in the extreme case, that there was no such thing as truth. What we call "truth" in this understanding is simply someone's *construction* of reality (not a *recognition* of reality), which is always biased — hence the notion that each of us has our own truth. For some postmodernists, "truth" is nothing more than a story that we tell to assert our power over others. In any case, with postmodernism, truth becomes (as they say) relative.

RELATIVISM

This explains, to a large degree, the state of our public discourse today. We rarely engage our opponents at the level of whether their claims are true or false. Such categories are less and less relevant. The question is not "Is this actually the case?" but rather "What is this person trying to gain by this assertion?" We live in a very suspicious age.

This is not to say that postmodernism is completely wrong. It is correct that truth is not the kind of thing modernism thought it was. It is even correct that many assertions of truth have hidden motives. Being aware of this is helpful. But postmodernism is an impossible thing to live by when taken to its logical conclusion, for at its core lies a deep contradiction. You cannot say things like "All truth is relative" or "We have no access to truth" or "Any pretense to truth is only a grasp at power" without asking your listener to believe that what you are saying is true!

Humans are built for truth and simply cannot avoid believing that certain things are true. If we pretend this is not what we are doing, we are being dishonest. We see, of course, people adept in postmodern theory who can deconstruct any number of previously accepted truths. But they do not leave the thrones they have tipped over empty. Instead, they immediately set them up again with new rulers as absolute as the ones so recently deposed. It is impossible — indeed, it is an oxymoron — to be an absolute relativist. Relativism is always selective.

Nevertheless, relativism is a very powerful narrative in contemporary culture, and it shapes popular discourse and opinion on a whole range of important questions. For instance, we often take for granted that there is no way to adjudicate between truth claims made by different religious traditions. We unthinkingly subscribe to the idea that all religions are equal paths to God. Until we don't. Because we do in fact encounter certain religious claims or practices that deeply disturb us: female circumcision, widows throwing themselves on the pyres of their husbands, even (in some circles) young-earth creationism. Then we need to convince ourselves that such things do not really represent the religion in question, or that such religions are, perhaps, not legitimate religions at all.

We manage to keep our religious relativism intact by ignoring what actual people believe and do and pretending that anyone with whom we really disagree doesn't actually represent their own religion. This is not to say that every religion is fully and accurately represented by its wildest fundamentalists, only that we are missing something if we unconsciously subscribe to a theory that makes any number of actual religious beliefs and practices not representative of any actual religion. Our relativism with respect to religion is necessarily selective.

And religion is just one area where relativism has taken a foothold. We often treat a person's political leanings as just a preference, unrelated to truth. Until we disagree with them! The same can be true of philosophy, or the arts. In a whole range of fields, we pay lip service to relativism until we feel strongly about something. What about education?

HOW TO THINK, NOT WHAT TO THINK

The medium is the message.

MARSHALL MCLUHAN

We often hear that we should teach students how to think, not what to think. And there is truth here. Teaching students what to think *without* teaching them how to think is dangerous and irresponsible. But let's look at this claim more closely. It says, on the one hand, that it is wrong to tell people what to think while, on the other hand, *telling us what to think* — namely, that it is bad to teach people what to think! To pretend to eschew truth claims while simultaneously making such claims is unavoidable for relativism.

Any education inevitably teaches people what to think. We cannot disentangle teaching how to think from specific content that is presented, however implicitly, as true. Teaching requires content. That does not mean teaching is reducible to communicating content. That, too, would be impossible. As the great Catholic communications theorist Marshall McLuhan learned from the doctrine of the Incarnation: The medium is the message. We can distinguish how to think and what to think, but we can never separate them completely. And to imagine we can is to think poorly.

To deny that we teach students what to think is disingenuous. When we do, the "what" in question is no longer recognized as content that could be challenged or investigated, critiqued, or nuanced, but is instead camouflaged as background assumptions about the way things are. It becomes the unacknowledged and unquestioned "neutral." And it is this kind of duplicity, not the open and honest acknowledgment of substantive positions and truth claims that we should have in Catholic schools, that is the necessary prerequisite for indoctrination.

INDOCTRINATION

Don't you see that the whole aim of Newspeak is to narrow the range of thought? In the end we shall make thought-crime literally impossible, because there will be no words in which to express it.

GEORGE ORWELL, 1984

Indoctrination feeds people a narrative and discourages or forbids any critical engagement with that narrative. This is *not* how Catholicism should be taught in Catholic schools. As we shall see in the next chapter, Catholicism has a long tradition of asking critical questions of itself in order to reach deeper understanding. Genuine faith does not discourage reasonable engagement, but welcomes it. If we really believe our truth claims, we should not be afraid of submitting them to honest critique. If they are true, they will come out more solid and compelling than before. If they are not, good riddance.

By definition, indoctrination avoids such critical engagement. It can do so by force, as when a totalitarian government explicitly forbids criticism. But it is usually done more subtly, controlling the language and categories in which we think in order to make it difficult to even imagine what critical engagement could look like. It works by making certain thoughts unthinkable.

People who have been subjected to this kind of indoctrination often consider themselves to be very critical thinkers, because they have learned to ask tough questions about all kinds of *other* worldviews. But they struggle to turn the critical lens back on their own views. And so, they easily imagine that no reasonable person could ever disagree with them. That both sides of the political spectrum in contemporary western democracies have gotten quite good at this kind of indoctrination goes a long way in explaining the state of our contemporary political discourse. Everyone can deconstruct every position but their own.

Contrary to its face-value appeal, relativism does not get us out of the difficult business of living and working with people who have radically different convictions from ours. Its pretense to neutrality actually makes this essential work *more difficult* because, by enabling different ideologies to smuggle in absolutist claims as if they are not claims at all, it makes conversation across divides next to impossible.

In a Catholic school, we do not need to be shy about teaching that what we believe is actually true out of a concern to respect the convictions of others. Everyone believes that what they believe is true, or they wouldn't believe it! Even if your belief is that people should keep their truth claims to themselves, you believe *it is true that people should keep their truth claims to themselves.* And you might even try to communicate that belief to other people and convince them to act accordingly!

The honest and respectful thing to do is to take responsibility for your truth claims by acknowledging them as such and to put them into constructive and critical dialogue with the corresponding claims of other people of good will. Don't resort to subterfuge, imposing your truth claims surreptitiously while pretending to neutrality. As a bonus, honest and constructive dialogue is much more likely to lead all parties involved to an encounter with truth than the word games we play to avoid having our truth claims recognized as such. In a Catholic school, we can both make our own claims boldly and unapologetically and engage in sincere and vigorous dialogue with those who disagree, including our students. Indeed, it is hard to imagine better training for participation in our pluralistic societies than such dialogue.

MAKE YOUR OWN MEANING?

A further consequence of the false neutrality that dominates our public discourse is the privatization of our exploration of humanity's deepest questions. We make a radical and far-reaching claim, while pretending to make no claim at all, when we assert (for example) that the answer to a question like "Does God exist?" is not important enough to impact one's convictions in public life. This attitude toward truth, an attitude that sidelines what humans have always considered to be life's most important questions, does not make the task of education easy. If a child has managed to take on the basic presuppositions of relativism by the age of eleven or twelve, it becomes very difficult to teach him much else. Why should he believe, or even engage with, the material we're presenting? Or any other material?

The brightest and most ambitious of these students quickly learn how to deconstruct everything in order to dismiss out of hand any claim or narrative that doesn't suit them. The rest don't bother. They just accept that, since everything is up for grabs and no real answers exist, all they can really strive for is to learn some technical skills that will give them a decent salary so they can afford a few creature comforts. The result of this sidelining of truth is some combination of anger, boredom, anxiety, and hopelessness. Sound familiar?

These answers do not satisfy the human heart. We are not

made for the endless deconstruction of the narratives that used to give us meaning. If there are important skills of deconstruction, and if there are in fact narratives that need deconstructing, that is because there is a true narrative we are meant to find. The idea that everything is up for grabs is sometimes presented as a positive. Because there is no meaning, we are "free" to make our own meaning. We unwittingly reinforce this when we tell kids, with all the good intentions in the world, that they can do or be anything. But are we perhaps feeding today's epidemic of teen anxiety?

Consider: If we can create our own meaning today, we can change it tomorrow. Deep down we know that we just made it up. What is more, an absence of meaning does not simply mean that we *can* make our own meaning, but that we *must*. This puts us in an impossible bind. Life is meaningless unless I give it meaning, but any meaning I can choose is always subject to revision and therefore unstable. Under such pressure, is it any wonder that some kids work themselves to exhaustion and others just give up? Our restless hearts need something much more real than that to rest in.

MADE WITH A MISSION

God has created me to do him some definite service; he has committed some work to me which he has not committed to another.

SAINT JOHN HENRY NEWMAN

God can make reality out of nothing, but we creatures are responsible to what already exists. We have creative powers, to be sure, but they are rooted in reality as it existed before we got here. To tell a child he can do anything he wants is, in the first instance, simply not true. There are countless things we can't do. There are thousands of jobs in which we would be unhappy and unhelpful. But what of it? God has created each of us with a purpose. We don't need to be able to do *anything*. We only need to find what we are called to do and do that. This story is both true and (because it is true) freeing.

Many young people find the idea that they can be or do anything more than just untrue; they find it paralyzing. It is not helpful to be told that I *can* do anything if there is no way to figure out what I *should* do. If the only determining factor is my own will and I am responsible to nothing beyond myself, any choice I make feels arbitrary. Rather than being empowered to choose by this attitude, many people simply delay or avoid choosing.

The contemporary crisis of commitment does not apply only to declining marriage rates and low numbers among those entering priesthood or religious life. It extends to the situations of countless young people who feel the need to "keep their options open" — those who, for example, keep going to back to school for one more degree or certificate, instead of launching out into the adult world. Or who, as Pete Davis lamented in his widely shared 2018 Harvard commencement speech, can't even commit to a whole movie on Netflix. Whether in work or in love, many young people today are paralyzed by this need to keep their options open.

The so-called freedom to do whatever we want is not experienced as freedom at all, but as shackles. We will never find the freedom we seek unless we are grounded in the truth of our own reality as creatures called by God to some great work. Catholic schools need to embrace this as the counternarrative to the anxiety-inducing notion that we must make our own meaning. It is only the truth about all of reality, above all about God and about ourselves, that will make us truly free.

PURSUING TRUTH

If a Catholic education is about making people more and more free — setting them free from false ideas, bad habits, untrue stories, and disordered loves — then it needs to believe in and pursue truth. And this needs to impact the whole curriculum. For in the background of every subject — from math to music, history to health — is a set of convictions about God and God's relationship to his creation, in particular to the pinnacle of that creation: the human person.

Nevertheless, the pursuit of truth is not an easy and uncomplicated matter. Postmodernity has shown us this to such a degree that many people assume it is impossible. But if postmodernity is wrong in the end (if, as we have seen, even it ends up unable to avoid making truth claims), then we need to think about just how we can pursue the truth. We need to take account of the relationship between the subjective human knower who pursues truth and the objective reality outside that knower to which he is responsible. If modernism ignored the subjective, postmodernism ignores the objective. If modernism sidelined freedom, postmodernism sidelines truth. For its part, Catholicism maintains that, if we want to give full scope to both the freedom of the knowing human subject and to the truth of the objective reality beyond ourselves, we need an appreciation of the complementary roles of faith and reason.

KEY TAKEAWAYS

Humans are built for truth and cannot avoid believing that some things are true. Relativism, therefore, is always selective.

Forthright and substantive truth claims are not indoctrination, but a protection against it.

Seeking for and finding the truth makes us free. Being told to make our own truth gives us a burden too great to bear.

Chapter 3
Faith and Reason

It is commonly suggested that faith and reason are mutually exclusive and even contradictory approaches to knowledge. The operative definition of faith in the atheist community, for instance, is something like "belief without reason" or even "against reason." The really troubling thing is that believers sometimes accept definitions like this without question. Let's be clear from the outset: This is not what "faith" means. Indeed, on this point Catholicism fully affirms the atheist assertion: You should never believe something *over against* reason.

The view that, for a good and faithful believer, faith has a kind of trump card over reason when the two appear to be in conflict is called fideism — literally "faith-ism" — and it has been officially condemned by the Church. Thinking that faith overrules reason is no more Catholic than believing reason overrules faith. For Catholics, apparent contradictions between faith and reason should be approached as an opportunity to seek deeper understanding, to discern whether one has perhaps misunderstood the claim of faith, or misused one's reason, or even a little of both. The Church might ask us to be humble about the state of our own understanding and to be open to learning more, but she never asks us to choose faith over reason or vice versa.

At the beginning of John's Gospel, we are told that "the word was made flesh." The Greek term typically translated as "word" is actually *logos*, which can mean not only "word" but "reason" as well. It shows up in English in the word "logic" and at the end of many terms we use to describe subjects of inquiry, from bio-logy to geo-logy to theo-logy. For Catholics, reason is rooted in God, and God does not ask us to abandon or ignore it, but to cultivate and employ it. Reason does not compete with faith, but cooperates with it.

It is hard to overstate the importance of understanding the relationship between faith and reason for Catholic education. When we get this wrong, the damage is incalculable. One of the key reasons young people give for abandoning their faith is that they have come to believe that it is unnecessary and even irresponsible to take things on faith. This often takes the form of saying that they "believe in science" or that they feel "science has replaced the need for religion" (something about which we will have more to say in the science chapter in Part II). Not only does confusion on this point lead to huge numbers of young people leaving the Church, it cripples the faith of those who remain. A faith that is not integrated with reason is often brittle and superficial, more a mark of identity than a satisfying approach to reality, and quite unequal to the challenges that life is sure to bring.

Imagining that faith and reason are opposed is a naïve approach to the question of how we know what we know. *Indeed, everything that we know, we know by the interplay of faith and reason.* In order to better understand this claim, we will need to look at what is often called "natural faith" — that is, the kind of basic belief and trust that we need in order to know anything at all and to function in our day-to-day lives, no matter what our religious commitments. This exploration will highlight just how superficial and misleading it is to claim that faith is opposed to reason. With this understanding in hand, we can then turn to the question of specifically Christian faith.

Natural faith is *analogous to* Christian faith. Analogies work by highlighting what different things have in common so that we can take what we know about one thing and use it to better understand another thing. Jesus used this method all the time by speaking in parables: "To what shall I compare the Kingdom of God? It is like …" But analogies only work if the two things at play are actually different. There are no "perfect analogies" because the only thing *exactly like* the thing you are trying to explain is that thing itself. And it is no help at all for Jesus to teach that "the Kingdom of God is like … um, well, you know, the Kingdom of God." If we want to use analogies well, we must attend to both the similarities and the differences involved. And so, while natural faith and Christian faith (also called "supernatural faith" or "the theological virtue of faith") have enough in common to both rightly be called "faith," we also need to notice what makes Christian faith unique. The most essential difference is this: While natural faith is simply unavoidable, Christian faith is a gift from God.

NATURAL FAITH

Believe so that you may understand.

SAINT AUGUSTINE

A simplistic view imagines that we know "religious" things by faith and "secular" things by reason. Therefore, the person who rejects faith as a way of knowing believes that they are simply opting out of religious knowledge, which is probably not valid or meaningful in any case. And both those who opt out of religious knowledge altogether and those who accept it but think it is unrelated to reason cannot see how faith could impact what we study in school beyond religion class. In this view, religion class involves faith, but all the other subject areas are the domain of reason.

But it is not only religious things that people know by faith, nor is it only religious people who know things by faith. All human knowing is done through a combination of faith and reason. This is just as true of mathematical knowledge as it is of religious knowledge. We cannot opt out of this. The human situation is such that reason always includes faith and is preceded by faith. As Saint Anselm put it, "I believe in order that I might understand."

This is because every act of human knowing necessarily begins with the presumption of things that cannot be strictly demonstrated by reason. For example, before we can know anything, we must presume that reality is intelligible, that some sense can be made of it, that we are not simply living with an illusion of knowability. Now, this is not an unreasonable thing to believe, but it *is* something that cannot be reasoned to in a strict sense. And the flip side of presuming that reality is *intelligible* is the presumption that we are *intelligent*. Not only is there sense to be made about reality, but we are the kinds of things that can make such sense. We presume that our thinking is not simply making up things that have no relationship to the way things actually are. To put it in the simplest terms: We have faith in our own reason. And it is reasonable to do so.

We also have faith in our senses. We believe that what we see, smell, hear, taste, and touch actually *is*. We cannot operate on a day-to-day basis without this presumption. And then there are the myriad things we constantly presume without double-checking or reasoning our way to them in everyday life: that the other drivers on the road have no intention of crossing the meridian, that the food from the grocery store is not poisoned, that most English-speakers use words to mean more or less what we mean by them. Without presumptions like these we would be paralyzed. It is simply not possible, nor is it *reasonable*, to live without some basic, more or less unproven, assumptions.

Now, notice that not all of these things work in exactly the same way. Presuming that reality is real and knowable is different in significant ways from presuming the goodwill of other drivers on the road. For instance, the latter of these is falsifiable in ways that the former is not. We can find out, in theory, if the milk is poisoned, but we are not in a strong position to discover if all of reality is just an illusion or if our reason is completely inadequate to it. Indeed, what would it mean to discover that reason was utterly inadequate to reality? We would need to do so using reason! In short, there are some things we take on faith that could be reached by reason, given adequate time, intelligence, and resources, but others that cannot be reached by reason, even in principle.*

---

*According to Catholic teaching, the existence of God can be known by reason alone. But it is OK that not everyone who believes in God has pursued the path of reason. Something true can be known by faith even if it is also demonstrable by reason. That God is Trinity, on the other hand, is something that can only be known by faith. We could never reason our way to the Trinity. But once God has revealed himself as Trinity, we can reason about the Trinity.

Notice also that we can be wrong in our presumptions. Faith isn't always correct just because it is faith. We know, for example, that some people actually have crossed meridians into opposing traffic. So, we take appropriate precautions if we see that another vehicle on the road is starting to drift. And we have all also experienced the failure of our senses to communicate the truth about reality accurately. We know about optical illusions or about various physical conditions that impair the functioning of our senses, from near-sightedness to feeling sensations in a limb that has been amputated. And anyone who has ever gotten less than 100 percent on a math test or lost a game of chess knows that human reason is fallible. Indeed, without careful training and attention, we are prone to being misled by all manner of logical fallacies. Humans make mistakes of reasoning all the time.

Note, however, that such errors do not cause us to abandon our faith in our senses or our reason. Rather, we use our senses and our reason to check themselves. If what I think I see makes no sense given what I know about the world, I double-check. I use my other senses, or some outside aid to my senses (like a flashlight, binoculars, a microscope, or even someone else's senses: "Do *you* smell something weird?") along with my reason to search for an explanation. Or, if I get a question wrong on a math test, I use my reason (often in consultation with the reason of a teacher, classmate, or parent) to come to understand my mistaken reasoning. As fallible as they are, our reason and our senses are basically reliable. More often than not, my eyes tell me what is really there. I get more math questions right than wrong, and I can usually come to understand how the ones I got wrong could be done correctly. Natural faith is not only unavoidable, it is reasonable.

FAITH AS TRUSTING RELIABLE SOURCES

Faith and reason are like two wings on which the human spirit rises to the contemplation of truth.

POPE ST. JOHN PAUL II

If I find (using my reason and my senses, notice) that one of my senses, or my reason in a particular area, is generally unreliable, I find workarounds, like trusting the reason or senses of others. Such trusting is not the use of reason itself, but it is far from unreasonable. Indeed, trusting the right kind of people — people with the right character, skills, and experience — is usually much more reasonable than trusting only our own reason or senses. This is why, for example, it is generally useful to trust authorities. If we are not lawyers, we tend to consult with them when a legal question becomes important in our lives. We do the same if we are not doctors, or structural engineers, or particle physicists, or child psychologists, or interior decorators. Of course, even lawyers check with other lawyers, as do all experts in their respective fields.

Furthermore, I only verify a tiny proportion of what I know about the world with my own reason and senses. There are vastly more things that I do not verify. How far away is England? What is the population of the earth? What is the speed of light? Does the earth go around the sun, or vice versa? Such things are, in theory, verifiable, but I don't verify them. I trust those who do. And it is reasonable to do so.

Of course, our faith in authorities can be misplaced. Authorities make honest mistakes. Sometimes they even intentionally mislead for things like personal gain or because of ideological prejudice. It is because of such things that we learn, even when we have a basic faith in authorities, to leave our critical faculties turned on. Genuine faith does not make one's beliefs impervious to reason but is always open to the feedback it gets from reason, ready to integrate new data for a fuller appreciation of the truth.

In this way, faith is purified. We can learn, for instance, that there are times and circumstances where we trust our senses or our reason or a given authority more or less completely, and other times when we need to think twice. We might learn that there are certain authorities we should never trust. We might learn that there are certain situations when our reason is very likely to fail (like during an emotionally charged argument) or our senses are unreliable (like when we are really tired). This does not mean having faith is irresponsible. What is irresponsible is insulating faith from reason and experience so that it cannot learn. Genuine faith does not close our minds, but opens them.

TRUSTING GOD

Fides quaerens intellectum
Faith seeking understanding

Saint Anselm's definition of theology

Christian faith is like natural faith in many ways. It believes things that cannot be known by reason alone but remains open to reason so as to grow ever closer to the truth. It does not contradict reason but empowers and frees reason to do its own proper work. And it trusts in reliable authority. But it is also unique. While natural faith is unavoidable if we want to know anything at all and to function in the world, Christian faith is a gift from God — what our Catholic tradition calls an "infused theological virtue" — given to us at baptism. And the content of that gift is a particular relationship of trust: With Christian faith, we are able to trust God, the most reliable authority, who reveals himself to us in love.

In human relationships, we can recognize an important difference between really knowing a person and simply knowing *about* a person. I might be able to learn lots of things about someone by doing a Google search. Or I can ask some mutual acquaintances for information. But if I have not met the person, and if he has not freely chosen to reveal himself to me, I do not say that I know him. In order for me to really know someone, he must disclose himself; and I need to trust in his self-disclosure. Without this, no interpersonal knowledge, and therefore no relationship, is possible.

God has revealed himself to humanity — in creation; in Israel, God's chosen people; and, finally and fully, in the life, death, and resurrection of Jesus Christ. It is possible for someone without Christian faith to know a lot *about* these claims of Christianity. But the faith we are given in baptism is the capacity to trust God's self-revelation in Jesus Christ. It is the capacity to be in a relationship of trust and intimacy so that we might know God and God's love for each of us in Christ.

This does not mean, by the way, that we always *feel* this way. Faith is not a feeling. Feelings come and go. Faith is a capacity to know the truth, and we can choose to engage that capacity through the freely given cooperation of our intellect and will. God's gift of faith does not coerce us, but enables us. It does not shut down our reason, but invites it out to play. Faith, as Saint Anselm's classic definition of theology teaches, always seeks understanding.

Consider the Annunciation. Mary was hearing from an angel of the Most High God (which is to say, from a trustworthy authority) something that did not make sense. She was going to have a baby. Now, Mary knew where babies come from. She also knew that she had not been involved with anything like that. And so she asked, "How can this be?" She did not, as someone might very understandably do, say, "This can't be!" Nor did she reject her perception ("I must be hallucinating!") or the content of the message ("I'm pretty sure you've got the wrong girl!"). Instead, she humbly inquired further into the meaning of the message. And Gabriel affirmed for her that this baby would not come about in the usual way. Because of the way Mary's faith sought understanding through the engagement of her reason, she has often been considered the Church's first theologian.

And what we see in Mary is exactly how a healthy relationship between faith — natural or supernatural — and reason works. When something or someone that we trust gives us new information, we work to integrate it into what we already believe to be true. This is the same whether an angel makes a birth announcement or an experiment in the lab shows an unexpected result. Sometimes integrating new information requires a radical rethinking of our previous understanding. Sometimes our previous understanding rightly leads to serious critical questions about the meaning or reliability of the new information. And pursuing such questions can lead to either integration or rejection of the new information. The process is not necessarily tidy. But what is required in each case is a kind of humility before the truth.

Genuine Christian faith does not lead to arrogance but is always deepening its relationship with the truth and integrating new information and insight into an ever more coherent and cohesive worldview. A faith that is unable to sustain this kind of rigor is a brittle faith that has little to offer either the believer or the world. It is not the theological virtue of faith our Tradition speaks of, but a false substitute — one wide open to the atheist critique that faith is really just an excuse to believe whatever one likes, without reference to reality.

Like natural faith, Christian faith is always in dialogue with our reason. In this way reason purifies our faith and keeps it from becoming mere superstition, resistant to reason, and unable to communicate with those who do not share it. And a recognition that reason itself relies on a kind of faith keeps reason humble and allows for genuine engagement with others who, while also committed to reason, do not share all our presuppositions.

FAITH AND REASON IN THE CLASSROOM

If, as we have argued, all human knowing is informed by both faith and reason, this will necessarily shape our teaching. Of course, what we have called natural faith will be present in every class. Without the presuppositions that our world actually exists and is not a dream or an illusion, that reality is intelligible and that we are capable of knowing true things about it, and that our reason and our senses are adequate to that task, we cannot even confidently assert that $2 + 2 = 4$. But what about our Catholic faith?

Like natural faith, a properly integrated Catholic faith also shapes the knowing that follows from it. Indeed, this is true of any kind of commitment about the way the world is. And everyone has such commitments. It may seem that, while natural faith is unavoidable, other kinds of faith are optional. Of course, that is true in a sense. But notice that you can only opt out of one such worldview by choosing another. No one gets to opt out of having some particular worldview and claim to occupy neutral ground from which to judge every other position. If someone pretends to such neutrality, she is simply blind to the nature of her own commitments. Though she might assume otherwise, the materialist is no better off here than the devotee of new age spirituality. Even agnostics have made commitments that are not neutral about what is and is not knowable.

In a public school that pretends to neutrality, all kinds of presuppositions will sneak in and inform how individual subjects are taught. In a Catholic school, we must not get caught in the same trap. If faith commitments are going to impact the classroom one way or another, teachers in a Catholic school need to be intentional that the faith commitments undergirding their teaching are Catholic. Catholicism needs to influence our approach to history and health, math and music, social studies and science. If Catholicism doesn't shape the way we teach every subject, something else will. Just *how* Catholicism can impact the way we teach every subject is the focus of Part II.

KEY TAKEAWAYS

Faith and reason are complementary — not contradictory — ways of knowing. All human knowing is done by a combination of faith and reason.

Faith is not just for religious people. Everyone believes at least some things by faith. This is often called natural faith.

Christian faith differs from natural faith in that it is a gift from God: a gift of a relationship of trusting God who reveals himself in love. Like natural faith, Christian faith is open and responsive to reason.

A properly integrated Catholic faith will inform how we approach all human knowing, including all the subjects we study in school.

Chapter 4
Catholicism Makes Everything Interesting

If all of human knowing is done through some combination of faith and reason, it is essential for Catholic teachers to consider the particular synthesis of Christian faith and reason, the worldview that follows from this synthesis, and its tremendous impact on human knowing and human culture. Indeed, it is difficult to imagine any worldview with a comparable impact across the whole range of human endeavors. As the American Catholic writer Walker Percy cheekily put it when asked about the reasons for his own conversion to Catholicism: "What else is there?"

In fields as diverse as philosophy, social outreach, art, literature, science, politics, law, healthcare, and education (to name just a few), the contributions of Catholic individuals, institutions, and religious orders have been decisive, even world-shaping. Consider names like Augustine, Dante, Mother Teresa and the Missionaries of Charity, Galileo Galilei, Caritas International, Dorothy Day, Thomas Aquinas, Sigrid Undset, Bartolomeo de las Casas, Michelangelo, Shusako Endo, Flannery O'Connor, Nicholas Copernicus, Gerard Manley Hopkins, Jacques and Raïssa Maritain, J. R. R. Tolkien, The Society of St. Vincent de Paul, Elizabeth Anscombe, Marshall McLuhan, Ignatius of Loyola and the Jesuits, Edith Stein, Georges Lemaître, perhaps, some argue, even Shakespeare. The fact that a list like this is completely inadequate and could be multiplied ten times over while still leaving out essential contributions is itself telling. And, if we permit ourselves to include the contributions of non-Catholic Christians like C. S. Lewis, William Wilberforce, Elizabeth Fry, Fyodor Dostoyevsky, Harriet Tubman, Desmond Tutu, Martin Luther King Jr., Corrie ten Boom, or Johann Sebastian Bach — people who were deeply shaped by the Gospel — the list is even more impressive. Even non-Christians, like Gandhi, have been deeply impacted by the Gospel in ways that have literally changed the world.

If a student graduates from a Catholic high school without having been given some sense of the breadth of the impact that Catholicism has had on the world, that is nothing less than a scandal. The names above, and dozens more, need to be in our curricula and our lesson plans, on posters on our walls and on our lips. While such a prodigious list is not in itself conclusive evidence of the truth of the Gospel, it is at least a compelling reason to take the claims of Catholicism seriously in a world where students are more likely to hear that their religion is obsolete bronze-age mythology than to be exposed to their own incomparable heritage.

Of course, no single book can adequately introduce the reader to the full range of Catholicism's contributions to culture and society. Indeed, the difficulty in writing the second part of this book was that each chapter could have easily become its own book. It was hard to be selective. The chapters in Part II are not intended to be the final word on any of the subjects discussed, but rather an introduction to thinking about them from a Catholic point of view. Each of us is responsible to continue our formation on this count, especially in our particular areas of expertise.

Being informed about Catholicism's rich social, intellectual, and artistic heritage is important. But it is also important to ask just what it is about Catholicism that produced such a heritage in the first place. If we want to convey a genuinely Catholic worldview in our teaching, we need to look deeper than a list of achievements and consider the context that nurtured such a list. As the steady flow of artistic and intellectual converts to the Church down through the ages demonstrates, Catholicism provides a deeply coherent and deeply beautiful vision of reality. It is a vision that, understood in its full depth, satisfies the human person — body, mind, and spirit.

And so, in our exploration of the various subjects in Part II, we will be interested not merely in listing and describing Catholic achievements, but in exploring a Catholic vision of the world as it applies to each subject. We want to come to understand just why it is that Catholicism makes everything interesting.

BOREDOM

Without a narrative, life has no meaning. Without meaning, learning has no purpose. Without a purpose, schools are houses of detention, not attention.

NEIL POSTMAN

One of the great challenges of education today is responding to meaninglessness and purposelessness. Public education, in particular, struggles to justify itself — at least to students — because it can offer no clear goals outside of the economic and the social. Such utilitarian goals are not enough to capture the imagination of young people. They might feel immense pressure to do well at school because of real or imagined economic and social consequences. But they are unlikely to be excited about learning because they find the material itself is fascinating. Indeed, teachers can perceive the sense of meaninglessness pervading much of contemporary culture, including education, in the boredom and distraction on the faces of their students. Teachers often report that students today are simply more and more bored.

The teacher imbued with a Catholic worldview will not be at all surprised at this. The reduction of all meaning to utilitarian concerns and personal preferences is bound to bore. People naturally ask, "What does it all mean?" To be told, or to have it implied, that it means nothing so you might as well do what you can to get ahead is deeply unsatisfying.

Worse, as we have seen in chapter 2, is to be told that we each get to (that is, *have to*) make our own meaning. A recent advertising campaign for cosmetics featured the tagline, "You are what you make up!" In the face of meaninglessness, we are to create our own meaning, like God, *ex nihilo* — out of nothing. While this is presented as a radical act of freedom, it is not experienced as genuinely creating meaning, but as destroying the very possibility of meaning. If I simply make something up, I know, deep down, that it is not true. I could change it tomorrow and change it again the next day. Anything that arbitrary cannot satisfy.

Indeed, not only does it not satisfy; it is the cause of great anxiety, as is obvious to any teacher today. When we tell young people to create their own meaning, purpose, and identity, we give them an impossible task. For whatever they decide might have been otherwise; that is, it might be wrong. But when you yourself are the supposed measure of all things, there is no way to know. Talk about laying heavy burdens and then not lifting a finger to help (see Mt 23:4)!

BUILT FOR TRUTH

It is gratifying to realize that, in our day too, the Christian vision, presented in its breadth and integrity, proves immensely appealing to the imagination, idealism and aspirations of the young, who have a right to encounter the faith in all its beauty, its intellectual richness and its radical demands.

POPE BENEDICT XVI

People need reference points outside of themselves if life is to mean anything. Or, to put it another way, humans are built for truth. We want to know what is really the case, not what we or someone else made up. Most of us, most of the time, would prefer to know an unpleasant truth than to believe a pleasant lie. And we intuitively recognize the tragedy of preferring falsehood. The genius of The Cardigans' hit song "Lovefool" is that it shows how sad and desperate a person who prefers falsehood to truth really is. None of us wants to be in the place of the singer who begs to be lied to — "fooled" — about her beloved's real feelings.

Even those sophisticates who tell us things like "all truth is relative," or "truth may exist, but we have no real access to it," or "any claims to truth are simply disguised claims to power," believe it is *true* that all truth is relative, that it is *true* that we have no real access to truth, that it is *true* that all claims to truth are claims to power. We are incorrigible. We seek truth even in the denial of truth. We can't help ourselves. We're built for it.

This deep conviction that humans are made for truth, that we thrive on it, is one of the underlying foundations of the Catholic vision of the world and therefore of Catholic education. Education is about the pursuit of truth because knowing who we are, who God is, and what this world God created is like are prerequisites for human flourishing, both here and hereafter. And, as we noted in chapter 2, once the notion of truth becomes problematized for students, education gets reduced to deconstructing the narratives that used to hold meaning or just learning enough technical skills to get a decent job. The real questions that make human life interesting and exciting are ignored. And boredom and cynicism set up shop.

The same commitment to truth that is at the foundation of a Catholic education is at the foundation of the Catholic intellectual heritage we highlighted at the beginning of this chapter. Catholicism makes everything interesting because, first of all, it insists that truth matters. Only from within a worldview that believes that truth is outside of myself and that I am responsible to it can such a wealth of intellectual excellence emerge. And, in addition to this insistence that truth exists and we can really know it, there are also particular truth claims of Catholicism that make art or math or health interesting. We will explore many of these in Part II. But, as we come to the end of Part I, let us consider some aspects of the Christian worldview that make certain subjects not just interesting, but possible.

A CHRISTIAN WORLDVIEW

It is hard for us to imagine that subjects like science or history, whose existence we take for granted, might not be. Of course, the things we *study* in science class (the natural world) and history class (the series of events in time) exist. But there have been times and places where what we call history and science — that is to say, *the frameworks we use for making sense* of the natural world and the series of events in time — either did not exist at all as conceptual categories or did not look very much like what we understand by those terms. Without the biblical worldview, the frameworks we take for granted for approaching knowledge in these areas could not have emerged. Science did not just happen everywhere that humans engage the natural world. It emerged only once, in a very specific context. It was no accident that its emergence was in Christian Europe. And the very meaning of the word *history* as we use it today has deep biblical roots. What is it about the Catholic worldview that led us to think of science and history the way we do?

At the heart of the Christian worldview is the biblical conviction that God is God and creation is not God. This might seem obvious, but it is actually quite radical. The transcendence of God — represented, for example, by the Old Testament image of the burning bush, where divinity irradiates but does not consume creation — has been a difficult thing for humanity to consistently uphold. We humans are generally tempted by various forms of pantheism that identify God with creation. The true idea that God is *in* everything easily becomes the false idea that God *is* everything; that there is no real distinction between God and the universe or between God and us. This is as true of ancient religious conceptions as it is of many modern ones. But Christianity, following Judaism, radically rejects such notions. And this has serious consequences for thinking about science and history.

SCIENCE

Why is God's transcendence important? First of all, it demythologizes the material world. Have you ever noticed what the Book of Genesis calls the sun and the moon? Simply "the greater light" and "the lesser light." Why? The first chapter of Genesis is an anti-Babylonian creation myth. The Jews were living in captivity in Babylon when Israel's creation story reached its final form, and in Babylon, as in a great many human cultures, the sun and moon were believed to be divine. The Jews needed to teach their children that only God was divine, and so they would not even name the sun and moon.

It is very tempting to worship the natural world. It is full of mystery and power. It sometimes behaves like a god whose wrath needs to be appeased. But once the material world is not worshiped as a god, it can be studied as a creature. And then you find that, the more you look into it, nature is not capricious and arbitrary but orderly and intelligible. The distinction between creature and Creator that the Judeo-Christian revelation insists upon is the deep root of what we call science.

HISTORY

Christianity is not one of the great things of history; it is history that is one of the great things of Christianity.

HENRI DE LUBAC

A second reason that God's transcendence is important for us is that it guarantees human freedom. The great problem of free will — how can humans be truly free if God is all-powerful? — is only resolvable if God's way of being is so different from creation's way of being that it is not in any competition with it whatsoever. When the early Church was trying to articulate its experience of Jesus in terms of Jesus' relationship to God, there was a ready-made option in the ancient world. That world knew about demi-gods, heroes like Hercules with a divine father and a human mother. The offspring of a Greek god and a human was semi-divine. That is because the Greek gods did not transcend creation. They were just as much a part of it as everything else and, while they were immensely powerful, they could not escape its basic laws. A Greek god interbreeding with a human was a bit like a horse and a donkey producing a mule. The result was a hybrid — odd, perhaps, but completely intelligible within worldly categories.

The Church rejected this option and instead said something heretofore unheard of. Jesus was not fifty percent human and fifty percent divine. He was *fully* human and *fully* divine. But that is only possible if humanity and divinity are such different *kinds* of things that they cannot be in competition. The difference between divinity and humanity is more like the difference between color and shape than the difference between two animal species that might interbreed. A ball can be fully red and fully round, because color and shape operate so differently from one another that they simply cannot be in competition.

Because God is so completely transcendent, his freedom is simply not in competition with our freedom. God is able to freely work through human freedom without overruling it. He shows us this in a stunning way on the cross. At Calvary humans have their way with God. He does not resist them. He tells Pilate explicitly that his Kingdom — that is, his power, his very way of being — is not of this world. Instead, Jesus is operating at a level that can absorb and transform human action. He does not need to overrule us. And so, God saves us *through* our own broken freedom, not by taking it away or defeating it, but by transcending it, which God can do only because he is even more free than we are.

Good parents and good teachers manage to image this in their best moments, freeing children to freely choose the good. Just think of the last time you were able to redirect a frustrated child instead of getting locked in a battle of wills. Notice, we can only do this when we are *more free* in the situation than the child we are freeing. If we are in unfreedom, we cannot.

Because God's transcendence allows creation to be creation, we have science. Because God's transcendence allows humans to be really free, we have history. If we do not believe in human freedom, we will not believe in history, at least not as we have come to use the word. Of course, we could still believe that events happen and that we can write them down and remember them. But "history" as we have come to know it means the possibility of something new, that freedom — human and divine! — can make a real difference. History is open-ended and responsive. It is something that can be shaped, not just recorded. History as we understand it is not simply a series of events in time; it is, in fact, as we will explore in chapter 6, the very opposite of fate.

EVERY SUBJECT

What about things like novels and autobiographies? Did we ever wonder where they came from? Or do we assume they, too, just *are*? Art forms also emerge in particular cultural matrices. Novels as we know them have a similar root to history. They are possible as an art form because of our biblical belief that humans are free and that our freedom is not arbitrary but directed to some real goal. And autobiographies — Saint Augustine's *Confessions* is often considered the first true autobiography — only exist in a culture that believes in the irreplaceable value of every individual human being.

Everyone believes some story about the world. It is impossible not to. And that story shapes how they view everything else. Moreover, every such story will involve the interplay of faith and reason. This does not mean that every story is equally true. People make mistakes of trusting and of reasoning all the time. Nor does it mean they are all false. One way to discern the truth of a story is to see how it all hangs together. What kind of worldview follows if this is true? If I believe this, what are the implications for everything else?

A Catholic education needs to answer this question. If Catholicism is true, what follows? It cannot be separated from the rest of life and learning. It will impact our understanding of science, of history, of math, of art, of health, of business, of sport, of ethics, of everything.

KEY TAKEAWAYS

Catholic teachers should familiarize themselves with Catholicism's intellectual and cultural heritage, especially in their area of teaching specialization.

It is important not only to know about the Catholic intellectual heritage, but to consider what it is about Catholicism that produces such a heritage.

The insistence that truth is outside myself and I am responsible to it is essential to cultural and intellectual excellence.

Subject areas like history and science are only conceived of the way they are today because of the influence of the biblical worldview, particularly the relationship between God and creation, on Western culture.

Part II
Catholic Academic Integration

The endeavor to interweave reason and faith, which has become the heart of individual subjects, makes for unity, articulation and coordination, bringing forth within what is learnt in school a Christian vision of the world, of life, of culture and of history. In the Catholic school's educational project there is no separation between time for learning

*and time for formation, between acquiring notions and
growing in wisdom. The various subjects do not present
only knowledge to be attained, but also values to be ac-
quired and truths to be discovered.*

CONGREGATION FOR CATHOLIC EDUCATION,
THE CATHOLIC SCHOOL ON THE THRESH-
OLD OF THE NEW MILLENNIUM

What makes an education Catholic? Is it enough to introduce religion class into an otherwise "neutral" curriculum? Does a crucifix in a science classroom make science class
Catholic? Are liturgies and service projects and a school ethos
that values every student as a child of God enough? According
to the Church: No! Of course, liturgies and service and ethos
and décor and religion class are all essential, and each deserves
our careful attention. But if the integration of Christian faith and
reason has not become "the heart of individual subjects," the education on offer is not yet fully Catholic.

As we emphasized throughout Part I, it is impossible to teach
any subject from a neutral point of view. A subject will be taught
with various presuppositions and commitments, intentionally or
not, which will shape the vision of life and reality that is impart-
ed to students. No one would dispute that, in a Jewish school,
for example, these presuppositions and commitments should be
Jewish. In a Catholic school, these presuppositions and commitments should be Catholic. The eight chapters of Part II are an
exploration of just how a Catholic worldview can impact our
approach to each subject under investigation. But, before we get
there, it is important to recognize that the idea that each subject
be taught from a Catholic point of view raises legitimate questions. What of the rightful autonomy of the subjects themselves?
Is each class to become just religion class in disguise? Is this not

more like indoctrination than education?

SCIENCE CLASS IS SCIENCE CLASS!

The Church does not forbid that "the human arts and disciplines use their own principles and their proper method, each in its own domain"; therefore, "acknowledging this just liberty," this Sacred Synod affirms the legitimate autonomy of human culture and especially of the sciences.

GAUDIUM ET SPES

It is essential, first of all, to emphasize that the Church does not ask Catholic teachers to transgress upon the rightful autonomy of individual disciplines. The methods proper to each subject must be acknowledged and respected. No theological claim gets to trump a claim proper to another discipline. This is why, for instance, in court cases about the teaching of Creationism in schools, Catholic experts are found testifying in favor of the teaching of evolution exclusively. Creationism (and its cousin, Intelligent Design) is not only bad science; by introducing claims about the miraculous into science class, it represents a fundamental methodological confusion. Students in a Catholic school should certainly learn about miracles. But they should never be given the impression that an appeal to miracles substitutes for legitimate scientific investigation. That is both bad scientific and bad theological method. Indeed, as we will see in more detail in chapter 8, it was the medieval Catholic theologians who insisted on the methodological independence of what was then called "natural philosophy" who first laid the theoretical groundwork for the scientific method.

Not only does a Catholic education preserve the rightful

autonomy of the sciences, it should prepare students to recognize when anyone is blurring the lines between the kinds of claims proper to science and other kinds of claims people make with or about science. The danger here goes in at least two directions. Sometimes doubt is cast upon the legitimate findings of science to serve a given ideology or interest (think of the efforts of Big Tobacco to confuse the public about the harms of smoking, for instance). Other times appeals to legitimate scientific findings are used illegitimately to short-circuit public debate in arenas like politics or healthcare, as if "following the science" always has straightforward and obvious applications in terms of policy. Recognizing the legitimate autonomy and limits of science is an essential part of having a solid scientific education. By helping us to properly locate scientific claims, Catholic faith should be part of the solution here, not part of the problem.

And what is true of science is true of every subject. Each should retain its own rightful autonomy, and each should recognize its own limits, contributing what is proper to it to a fully integrated worldview. A Catholic approach should not undermine this dynamic, but undergird it. Catholic Academic Integration is about making sense of the world with the legitimate input of the disciplines — constructing a beautiful and coherent synthesis informed by faith *and* reason — not about constraining those disciplines to fit into some narrow box. Indeed, *that* would be a form of fideism, an error which, as we saw in chapter 3, has been officially condemned by the Church. Properly understood, the Catholic faith does not circumscribe our encounter with reality, but opens us to the truth found anywhere and everywhere.

CONTENT AND CONTEXT

So, what makes a Catholic school different from any other place where people look for truth? The difference is not in what truths are allowed to be seen. The difference is the supernatural light in which all truths are seen, the light of God that illuminates them.

CHRISTOPHER BAGLOW

It is also important to recognize that Catholic Academic Integration is not primarily about adding Catholic content. Of course, in certain classes (like Literature, Music, and Art), Catholic content can and should be studied in a Catholic school. But by no means exclusively. It is essential that students encounter great Catholic art and artists, but it is also essential that they learn how to approach all art, no matter who produced it, in a Catholic way. We need to teach not merely Catholic content, but teach from within a Catholic context for making sense of all life and learning.

In other classes, of course, specifically Catholic content can be harder to come by. And forcing Catholic content in can feel artificial and contrived. Math problems about years in purgatory are more likely to generate eye rolls than deep Catholic convictions. Arbitrary Catholic content that is not integrated in a Catholic worldview might even lead to resentment at feeling brainwashed. Of course, there may be important Catholic contributions in the history of subjects like math and science, and students in Catholic schools should learn about them. But the fact that the Big Bang was proposed by a Catholic priest does not change the scientific content or value of that proposal. Catholics don't believe in the Big Bang because it was proposed by a priest, but because it is the best scientific explanation currently available. That a priest proposed it tells us a lot about Catholicism. It tells us next to nothing about astrophysics.

But even in a math class, where specifically Catholic content is hard to imagine, the Catholic context of math class matters. This is because the way we teach math answers a whole host of deeper questions beyond mathematical content. For example, what are the implications of the fact that creation is so orderly that a whole language and symbol set (math!) can be developed and refined ever more precisely to describe it and never run into self-contradiction? Why, that is, does creation make so much sense? And what does it mean that humans are the kinds of creatures that do math? We've never yet encountered other beings that relate to reality in this way, probing the secrets of the universe for practical purposes, yes, but also for the sheer joy of it. What does the practice of math say about us? What does it mean that we treat things, like the number nine, as if they exist, even though no one could ever show you a nine existing independently in nature? What kind of reality, in other words, do things that have no material existence of their own have? What are the goals of math? Why should people learn it? If math is good and being skilled at math is good, is everything done with math good? None of these are math questions. They are questions about *what math means.*

From a Catholic point of view, math teaches us that God creates an orderly and coherent universe. The Creator of the universe is not whimsical or capricious, as pagan gods are often depicted. God does not toy with us. Which is not to say that God is always predictable. God is both coherent *and* full of surprises. Like math! That humans do math also tells us a lot about ourselves: that we are naturally inclined to seek to understand the world around us; that we have immense powers of understanding that we can use for good or ill; that we are made not only for the concrete and the material, but for the abstract and the spiritual; even that we ourselves are microcosms of a creation that includes both the concrete and the abstract, the material and the spiritual, and that those things relate in interesting and subtle ways that are worth considering.

Now, don't imagine that a math class that never deals with these kinds of things explicitly isn't communicating something about them implicitly. Even a math class that only manages to convey that such matters are an idle waste of time communicates something very powerful. And very false! As we have said, every subject is always taught from a particular point of view. And the most naïve and uncritical point of view is the one that imagines itself to be simply neutral. To ignore underlying questions of context and worldview is simply to provide very poor answers to those questions. It does not actually leave them open.

Indeed, for just this reason, Catholic Academic Integration is quite the opposite of indoctrination. Pretense to neutrality is always the prerequisite for indoctrination. Naming and owning one's point of view openly, on the other hand, allows for freedom, dialogue, and even healthy, honest, and productive disagreement. Teaching everything from a Catholic point of view does not mean that students who do not accept that point of view, in whole or in part, cannot do well in class. It means that every student will be responsible for thinking critically about their own point of view and how it relates to a Catholic one and learning how to communicate honestly and respectfully with other points of view. That's a pretty important skill these days.

DEVELOPING YOUR OWN CATHOLIC WORLDVIEW

Of course, when seeking to teach from a Catholic point of view, there is no substitute for being steeped in that worldview yourself. And so, the most important prerequisite for teaching all subjects from a Catholic point of view is to take an active interest in our own intellectual (as well as spiritual) formation as Catholics. If you specialize in a given subject, you should be increasing your expertise as a *Catholic* teacher in that subject. Catholic English teachers should know the Catholic literary canon. Catholic science teachers should know the Catholic history of modern science and be equipped to deal with common misunderstandings about faith and science, like those around evolution. Catholic physical education teachers should have studied and considered what their faith teaches about healthy and disabled bodies, or about the virtues encouraged by exercise and sports.

This can't all be done in one short book. It is the work of a lifetime. Nevertheless, in the second part of this book, we will look at eight key subject areas and consider how a Catholic point of view will influence our approach to them in the classroom. Think of this work as putting on a new pair of glasses. For many of us, the very idea that subjects other than religion can and should be taught from a Catholic point of view is surprising. Hopefully this idea is starting to make sense. What is offered in the rest of this book is a way to begin looking at each subject under consideration with Catholic eyes. It is not a matter of making teachers responsible for more and more content, but of giving them the lenses to see how Catholicism can inform how they teach everything. When you get new glasses, there is usually a period of adjustment. But once you get used to them, you hardly notice they're there. Once you have learned to view your subject with Catholic lenses, Catholic Academic Integration becomes almost automatic.

MAKING THE MOST OF PART II

While Part II includes some practical ideas for the classroom, this book is not a curriculum or a collection of lesson plans. As we explore our eight key subject areas from a Catholic perspective, we will also learn to recognize many of the unacknowledged cultural presuppositions that often inform the presentation of these subjects and that run counter to our Catholic faith. By helping you to hone your own Catholic worldview, this book should equip you to integrate the Catholic faith into your classroom. To help move from this book to your classroom practice, here are some questions to consider after each chapter in Part II. If you are reading this book with your staff or for a class, they can serve as discussion questions with colleagues or classmates.

- Where do the ideas in this chapter intersect with the curriculum I am responsible for teaching?
- What in this chapter affirmed or clarified something I already believed as a Catholic? Was there anything in this chapter that I found surprising or had questions about?
- Am I better able to recognize elements of a non-Catholic point of view in my subject area? Can I remember any times when such elements showed up in my school or classroom through students, parents, resources, etc.? How might I address those elements?
- Can I think of any unit or lesson plans I would change having read this chapter? How would I change them? Can I think of any assignments I could create (or tweak) to reinforce a Catholic worldview in this subject area?

KEY TAKEAWAYS

Catholic Academic Integration does not mean that theology should transgress the appropriate methodological independence and integrity of the disciplines.

Catholic Academic Integration includes adding Catholic content to classes but must not be limited to that. Teaching every subject from within a Catholic context is even more important.

Openly acknowledging the viewpoint from which we teach does not shut down other viewpoints, but allows for open, honest, and critical engagement.

Catholic Academic Integration is not about giving teachers more tasks, but about giving them new lenses for the tasks they are already doing.

Chapter 5
Literature and Language Arts

Humans are storytelling creatures. We try to make sense of our world and of ourselves through stories. Every good preacher knows this and tries to convey the truths of the Gospel through stories. Jesus himself was such an effective storyteller that people remembered his stories well enough to write them down decades after he first told them, and the works containing those stories — which we call the Gospels — have transformed human self-understanding and human history. Effective politicians know that stories are essential for communicating their message to the people they want to reach. So do advertisers. Children beg their parents for stories, and parents who want to raise their children well know that they had better give them what they ask for. If we are to live a full life, oriented to the good, the true, and the beautiful, good stories are indispensable.

This is why the study of literature is essential to any education worthy of the name. But the study of literature is itself embedded in the study of language more generally. We are storytelling creatures, but we can only be so because we have been endowed with language. Indeed, many have argued that the emergence of abstract language is what marks human beings off from our prehuman ancestors. And some theologians speculate that evidence of language might be the closest thing we can find to archeological evidence of God giving humans rational souls. Being immaterial, souls can leave no physical trace of themselves. But language — thought become sound and then the written word — is perhaps the clearest example we have of the immaterial impacting the material. Which is why the Bible loves to use language as a metaphor for God's relationship with creation. From the stories of creation in Genesis to the prologue of John's Gospel, words are always becoming flesh and dwelling among us.

Many animals, from bumble bees to killer whales, have impressive forms of communication that enable them to cooperate and accomplish more as a group than they ever could as individuals. But human language is of another order. Human language is capable of abstraction. Humans, like killer whales, can cooperate in a successful hunt. But killer whales don't use language to consider what it means to use language, as we are doing right now! Indeed, it is this unique characteristic of human language that allows us to abstract to the point of recognizing that the universe does not account for its own existence and that reality is more than our immediate relationship with our material surroundings. As Joseph Ratzinger has argued, our ancestors became human precisely when they became capable of the thought: "God."

To study literature and language arts, then, is to dive deep into what we are as human creatures. Endowed with language, humans incessantly pursue meaning, not just through the stories we tell about ourselves, but even through the basic ordering of our language into meaningful units. That is to say, before we get to *explore meaning* through literature, we have to be able to *make meaning* with grammar. Nothing is true — or good, or beautiful — that is not first coherent.

As much as any other subject we study in school, literature gives us the possibility of incredibly rich Catholic content. Catholic poets, novelists, dramatists, and short story writers are among the best in the world and rightfully take their place even in the curricula of public schools. No one should graduate from a Catholic high school without having been given some exposure to their own literary heritage as Catholics. But, as you probably suspect by now, we will not be satisfied with simply adding Catholic content to our Language Arts classes. We must also ask deeper questions. What is it about Catholicism that produces such great literature? How can we, as Catholics, fruitfully read and engage with non-Catholic literature? And, finally, what does a Catholic worldview have to say to us about language more generally and its role in human life and culture?

KNOWING THE CATHOLIC
LITERARY HERITAGE

The Catholic novelist doesn't have to be a saint; he doesn't even have to be a Catholic; he does, unfortunately, have to be a novelist.

FLANNERY O'CONNOR

It should be a point of professional pride for any Catholic English teacher to cultivate a deep familiarity with and appreciation for the Catholic literary heritage. This is not meant to be exclusive. Of course, we want Catholic teachers with a whole range of expertise, inside and outside the Catholic tradition. And we need to teach how to engage with non-Catholic literature as well, as we will explore in the next section. That said, names like Tolkien, O'Connor, Percy, Hopkins, Undset, or Chesterton should be as familiar as old friends to English teachers, and no one should graduate from a Catholic high school without having heard of them.

If such authors are already in your curriculum, great! Take the time to develop your own expertise in their life and work so that you can present them with verve and imagination. Even in a public school, it would be appropriate to explore how a given author's religious faith impacts their artistic vision. In a Catholic school, with Catholic authors, it should be a given. Moreover, many of these writers have not only written great works of literature, but they have written *about literature* in illuminating ways. Reading selected letters from Flannery O'Connor after one of her short stories or looking at Tolkien's ideas about fairy stories as a genre after reading his novels will deepen the students' experience of the literature itself and of the Catholic imagination underlying it. (But take the "after" seriously. It is important to let the works speak for themselves upon first reading. Let's not rob students of the experience of literature for its own sake.)

If none of these authors appear in your curriculum, make it your business to find places to fit them in. In Canada, for instance, where three provincial Catholic school systems are publicly funded and share curricula with public schools, there remains significant flexibility to choose literature within broad parameters. Whether by genre or by theme, it is not hard to find a place for novels such as *A Canticle for Leibowitz* or poems like "As Kingfishers Catch Fire." Giving the teacher even more flexibility is the fact that there has been very good Catholic literature — by which I mean literature expressive of a Catholic worldview —

produced by non-Catholics! This is most obviously the case with literature written by other Christians whose worldview overlaps to a great degree with Catholicism. C. S. Lewis, an Anglican, is a prime example. The Eastern Orthodox Fyodor Dostoyevsky wrote profoundly Christian works. But even authors with ambiguous relationships to Christianity like Willa Cather and Ethel Mannin have produced great Catholic novels. We will touch on this phenomenon briefly below. Our purpose here is merely to point out the wide range of great literature available to teachers looking to augment the Catholic content of their English class. A Catholic worldview is such fertile soil for the imagination that it fosters artistic creativity well beyond the visible bounds of the Church itself. And so, in addition to introducing students to their Catholic literary heritage, a truly Catholic Language Arts class will explore just what it is about Catholicism that makes it so creative.

WHY DOES CATHOLICISM PRODUCE SO MUCH GOOD LITERATURE?

It is valuable, when studying any literary work, to seek to understand the cultural context and worldview of its author. *Paradise Lost* cannot be rightly appreciated without reference to Milton's British puritanism. Nor can *The Iliad* or *The Odyssey* be properly understood if Homer's ancient Greek cultural and religious background is unknown to the reader. Even Scripture is no exception here, and our reading of it is greatly aided by knowledge of the histories and worldviews of the people whom God employed to produce it. This is why, as we noted above, it is appropriate even in non-Catholic schools to explore the religious worldview of any Catholic authors being studied.

The reverse is also true. That is, we can learn a lot about a culture or worldview by looking at the kind of literature it produces. So, in addition to teaching the Catholic backgrounds of authors like O'Connor and Tolkien, we should ask why Catholicism produces writers like O'Connor and Tolkien in the first place. What is it about Catholicism that leads to great literature? Exploring this question will lead us to a deeper appreciation of both our faith and its literature.

There are several intertwined elements of Catholic belief that contribute to a Catholic literary imagination. We will look at five key factors in particular, but this list does not pretend to be exhaustive. First, we believe in the Bible, which is to say, we believe God chose *a collection of literature* to communicate his message of salvation to us. Second, our theology of creation recognizes and communicates the awesome power of language. Third, the Incarnation of Jesus doubles down on the biblical emphasis on the power of language. Fourth, the sacraments of the Church teach us that even everyday items and activities are part of God's plan and story, and they have more meaning than we might at first suspect. Finally, and following from our theology of creation and Incarnation, we believe that human persons are intrinsically, even infinitely, valuable and interesting. We will look at a sixth consideration — belief in objective truth — in chapter 12 because it applies to all of art, though it certainly contributes to good literature and a Catholic literary imagination.

THE BIBLE

If humans are indeed storytelling animals, it is not a surprise that God would communicate with us through stories. This is just as true of Jesus telling stories to teach his audience as it is of the creation stories in the Book of Genesis. Moreover, the Bible is not just a collection of stories such as parables and creation myths, it is itself one overarching story of God's relationship with humanity, from creation and fall to redemption and glory. In a biblical culture, people learn to identify themselves as participants in a grand story that is both bigger than they are and also intimately concerned with them. Life is not meaningless, but is oriented to fulfillment. And, as small as we seem in the wide world, we are of infinite concern to God. Like all our favorite Bible characters, our own longings and hopes, fears and failures are taken up into God's story and redeemed there. The Bible teaches us that we are made not just for a happy ending, but a glorious one. This biblical sense of history itself being, above all, God's story infuses the Catholic imagination with the sense that stories matter, and that truth is to be found in them. They are not merely things we tell to entertain ourselves or to pass the time, but they are intimately connected with our lives, our identities, and our destiny. How could such a vision *not* inspire literature?

Moreover, the simple fact that we believe God can speak to humanity through the Bible means that Catholics trust in the power of words. Language is capable of conveying truth. This is no small thing. Many people are skeptical on this point. Some suggest there is no truth, others that, even if there is truth, it is not accessible to us. Some believe that any use of language is always just an attempt to gain power over others. As Catholics, we do not deny that language can be abused in this way. Nor do we imagine that language can easily and straightforwardly assert every true thing or that there is no gap at all between the truth itself and the words used to try to express it. But neither the possibility of manipulation nor the reality of mystery leads us to conclude that language cannot express truth. Instead, both invite us to use language with great care and reverence, recognizing its power and its limits. Again, how could such an attitude *not* inspire the literary imagination?

CREATION

And God said, "Let there be light;" and there was light.

GENESIS 1:3

One of the most fascinating elements of the biblical story of creation, one that we might even miss due to overfamiliarity, is that God creates by speaking; that is to say, God creates *with words*. As we have seen, the final version of the Book of Genesis was put together in Babylon, where the Jews were living in exile. And an important function of the Jewish mythology at the time was to counter the mythology of their captors. In Babylonian mythology, the god Marduk had created the world by slaying a great sea monster, Tiamat, and had fashioned human beings from her entrails to be slaves to the gods. The true depth of the Bible's theology of creation becomes clearer for us when we read the first chapters of Genesis as the repudiation of such a vision. The notion that human beings are made in God's image and likeness takes on more meaning, for example, when we see it against the backdrop of the Babylonian view of humanity as slaves. We will return to this theme below. But let us first consider this creation with words.

Notice that the God of the Bible does not struggle against a rival the way Marduk does. The God of the Bible has no rival. To be able to speak things into being, rather than having to conquer them in battle, is to be in a peaceful and transcendent relationship with creation. The biblical God, in other words, is a different kind of god altogether. But the fact that the Bible prefers the metaphor of speech to the metaphor of battle for the act of creation indicates something else as well. It implicitly recognizes the intrinsic relationship between human language and human culture. It teaches, in short, that *words create worlds*.

Think about the function of words and language in forming

your own world. We are all so utterly shaped by our mother tongue that we rarely even notice its impact on our way of thinking and being until we try to learn another language. And each of us can probably remember words of affirmation from a parent, teacher, or coach that profoundly shaped our sense of self. We can also probably think of words of accusation or insult that have wounded us deeply. Or think of your favorite books and how your life might be different if you had never read them. The biblical image of God speaking the world into existence is far from arbitrary. It reflects the deep truth that human reality is created by language.

And the Genesis stories continue to reflect on the role of language even beyond the act of creation. God does not simply create with words; he pronounces his creation "very good." Like any good father, God *affirms* with words. Even the role of evil is presented as a corruption of language. In Babylonian myth, Marduk did battle with a great serpent. In Genesis, the serpent is not God's rival in combat, but a crafty sneak, one whose weapons are twisted words. If God's words create and affirm, then the enemy of God can only be "a liar and the father of lies" (Jn 8:44). Any worldview that takes language this seriously in its story of creation is bound to produce great literature.

THE INCARNATION

In the beginning was the Word.

JOHN 1:1

The Gospel of John begins with the same phrase as the Book of Genesis: "In the beginning." For John, the Incarnation is the recapitulation and fulfillment of creation. Jesus is humanity as originally intended by God. In Jesus, one man will finally live a whole life of unbroken communion with God — God's intention for all of creation from the beginning. Consider Pilate's words during Jesus' trial, "Behold the man." Here, in Jesus, is man as intended by God. Incarnation follows upon and, in a sense, completes creation. And so, it follows that if our doctrine of creation fosters art and literature, our belief in the Incarnation encourages this dynamic even further.

In the prologue to his Gospel, John takes the image of God's creation through speech from Genesis and gives it a shocking depth: "In the beginning was the Word, and the Word was with God, and the Word was God. He was in the beginning with God. All things came into being through him, and without him not one thing came into being" (1:1–3). The very Word that "became flesh and lived among us" (1:14) in the Incarnation is the same Word through whom God created all that is. The continuity between creation and Incarnation is palpable here.

Moreover, as in the creation stories, we see the power of words continually on display throughout the Incarnation. We see again God the Father using words of affirmation: "This is my Son, the Beloved, with whom I am well pleased" (Mt 3:17). It is hard to imagine more powerful words from a father to a child. Every son and daughter longs for just such affirmation from their dad. And it feels quite inadequate to choose only a few examples of Jesus' incredibly powerful words. To the woman caught in adultery: "Has no one condemned you? ... Neither do I condemn you. Go your way, and from now on do not sin again" (Jn 8:10–11). To the Pharisees asking about his authority (and to the paralyzed man at the center of the controversy): "But so that you may know that the Son of Man has authority on earth to forgive sins ... I say to you, stand up and take your bed and go to your home" (Lk 5:24; see Mt 9:6). To Peter, after his betrayal: "Do you love me... ? ... Do you love me? ... Do you love me?" (Jn 21:15–17). The power of Jesus' speech was put remarkably by

Peter in John 6 after the stunning Bread of Life discourse: "You have the words of eternal life" (v. 68). Have we ever considered, not just that Jesus had such words, but that words are even the kinds of things that can be "of eternal life"? What power there is in words!

Every English classroom in every Catholic high school should have some kind of "In the beginning was the Word" poster on prominent display. And could we not explore the foundational role of words in human reality that we see in the Scriptures with assignments that reflect upon the impact that words have had on people and on history? When totalitarian governments feel the need to censor speech, they are offering a forceful affirmation of an Incarnational theology of language. As the Resurrection makes clear, once words have become flesh, the powers of this world have a very hard time killing them and keeping them in the tomb!

A SACRAMENTAL IMAGINATION

Moreover, God joining creation in the Incarnation taught us that God comes to us every day in the material, created order. God cleanses us with water, feeds us with bread and wine, anoints us with oil. Every bath is a preparation for meeting the divine. Every meal is an anticipation of a heavenly banquet. The universe, right down to simple daily human activity, is charged with meaning and points beyond itself to something more. All of creation is a symbol of God's love and providential care. This Catholic attitude is often called a "sacramental imagination." In the seven sacraments of the Church, God chooses some element of the created order to convey his grace to us. But it is also true, in a more general way, that the whole universe is a sacrament, pointing beyond itself to its Creator and conveying God's grace to us through meeting our needs or stunning us with beauty. And it is the Incarnation that is the linchpin connecting creation and the sacraments. Jesus' humanity, his participation in the material and historical order, is itself a sacrament, at once manifesting God's presence in time and space and pointing beyond time and space into eternity: "Whoever has seen me has seen the Father" (Jn 14:9).

In the Incarnation, Jesus did not only speak, he acted in the physical world. He made paste out of dirt and saliva and spread it on a blind man's eyes. He touched lepers. He broke bread. And he spoke as he did so, giving instruction, affirmation, and blessing. As every great novelist and poet knows, this combination of language and symbol is stronger than either alone. Symbols give depth to words beyond what words convey on their own. Words give clarity to symbol, helping us to interpret them aright. When we do "show *and* tell," we are imitating God.

Theologians speak of "form" and "matter" in the Church's sacraments. The form is the words used in the celebration (e.g., "This is my body" or "I baptize you in the name of the Father and of the Son and of the Holy Spirit"). Such words are incredibly powerful. They effect what they say. When a priest pronounces these words, bread really does become Christ's Body and a person really is washed free from sin and incorporated into (that is, literally, brought into *the Body* of) Christ and his Church. Such effectiveness does not depend on the words alone, but on the physical symbols and actions that accompany them, what theologians call the "matter" of the sacraments. If there is no bread present, there is no Eucharist, no matter what the priest says. If there is no water, no one is baptized, no matter what the priest says. There must be, in other words, some "flesh," some element of material reality, for the words to shape and inhabit. Words are powerful, and they are more powerful the more they are able to become flesh. An author steeped in this sacramental vision of the world, who instinctively sees meaning in the everyday, who senses God's presence and purpose in all of creation, who intuits the power of a carefully crafted symbol, is an author well-equipped to tell stories that matter, stories that help us to recognize the beauty and grandeur, the potential and the significance of our own lives.

EVERY HUMAN PERSON IS INFINITELY VALUABLE

You have never talked to a mere mortal.

C. S. LEWIS

Remember the Babylonian creation story? The one in which humans were created as slaves for the gods from the guts of a monster? As repugnant as this seems, we should recognize that stories that justify the power of the few over the many, or stories that imagine everyone outside the group as lesser, are everywhere. We are aware, of course, of egregious examples like Nazi propaganda or the justifications of race-based slavery. But the more basic attitude here is indicated in something as simple as the fact that the names ethnic groups give themselves often mean simply "the people." Conversely, the ancient Greeks called all outsiders, that is, those who did not speak Greek, "barbarians" in reference to their unintelligible speech. Generally speaking, cultures have different rules for members than for foreigners in ways that are often unjustified or prejudicial.

If we are unaware of this, it is hard for us to see what a revolution biblical religion constitutes in human history. Contrary to the Babylonian myth, in the Bible, humans are created in God's image and likeness for love and for freedom. Throughout the Old Testament, Israel is admonished to treat the slave, the foreigner, the widow, and the orphan with justice, remembering their own history of slavery in a foreign nation. For all its seeming concern with tribal purity, the Old Testament is constantly telling stories of non-Israelites being incorporated into God's chosen people. This pattern is underscored in the genealogy at the beginning of Matthew's Gospel, which traces Jesus' lineage, father to son, from Abraham. Not including Mary, the genealogy names the mother only four times, and in each instance — Tamar, Rahab, Ruth, and Bathsheba — the woman is not an Israelite.

The Book of Jonah is stunning, even comical, in this regard. Jonah hates Nineveh and the Ninevites, and he hopes that God will destroy them but is frustrated because he knows that God is too merciful to do so. Most prophets despair that their message is not heeded; Jonah despairs when his *is* heeded and God spares the city. God admonishes Jonah, "And should I not be concerned about Nineveh, that great city, in which there are more than a hundred and twenty thousand persons who do not know their right hand from their left, and also many animals?" (4:11).

Jesus' ministry, of course, exemplifies this universal love of God. He ministers to Samaritans (sworn enemies of the Jewish people), heals a Gerasene (people who keep unclean pigs!), and even revives the daughter of a Roman military officer (a representative of the very empire occupying Jesus' homeland). He dies on the cross for all, Jews and Gentiles alike, as the inscription above him, in Hebrew, Greek, and Latin, makes clear. And the message of the Gospel goes out from Jerusalem — first to Samaria (of all places!), then to the known world.

The biblical message is as clear as it is unusual: Every human person is created and loved by God. Every single person matters to God. If this seems obvious to us, we should recognize two things. First, this has not been obvious to most humans for most of history, but is actually a revolution. In fact, a major concern with the promulgation of the United Nations' Universal Declaration of Human Rights, deeply influenced by the work of Catholic philosopher Jacques Maritain, was that it not be perceived as the imposition of Christian values on the world! The second thing to recognize is that even those of us who think we know and believe in the dignity and equality of every human person need to be aware of just how easy it is to speak and act as if some people are worth less than others. The temptation to dehumanize others can take on very subtle forms and is excused in a thousand ways. Seeing every person as a beloved child of God is the work of a lifetime.

But what does this have to do with literature? Implicit in the notion that every person is created and loved by God, indeed made for eternity with God, is the sense that every person is *interesting*. The street urchin and the slave and the day laborer and the housewife and the spinster and the prisoner and the desk jockey and everyone else you care to list is a creature intended by God for glory. The Christian is convinced, then, that every single person has a story that matters. Humans are fascinating.

Indeed, it is the Christian fascination with the individual human person that has led not simply to some good books, but to the development of at least two genres of literature. Both the autobiography and, especially, the novel are fundamentally Christian art forms. This is because both these literary forms are premised on the notion that human lives and human experiences have about them something universal and interesting. Human experience is communicable. We have enough in common to be able to put ourselves in the shoes of another person and genuinely understand them. More than that, when we understand others, we better understand ourselves!

Many autobiographies, especially the ones that sell well enough for us to be familiar with them, are written by famous people. But there are also many great autobiographies of people whose stories were largely unknown before publication. And novels in particular are interested in the basic experiences of humanity and are very often accounts of the lives of "ordinary" people. Such autobiographies and novels play a significant role in teaching us that such people are not really ordinary at all. There is enough tragedy and enough glory in every human story to write a book. If we doubt this, the best cure is to learn to look at our own stories through the eyes of God, who sees in each human person the striving for eternity in the face of a broken and sinful world that is the basic drama of human life. We all have a story worth telling.

The great novelists are, above all, great observers of humanity. They see the universality of human nature and of the human struggle. It is this essentially Christian vision that enables these writers to convey the truth about us in stories about people who live continents and centuries away from us. The novel, as a literary form, conceives of humanity the way Christian revelation does, as oriented to something beyond ourselves, in pursuit of something, on the way, *in via*. And we know, as Catholics, that the ultimate goal of that pursuit is nothing less than God.

SEEDS OF THE WORD: STUDYING NON-CATHOLIC LITERATURE

Even beyond its typically religious expressions, true art has a close affinity with the world of faith, so that, even in situations where culture and the Church are far apart, art remains a kind of bridge to religious experience.

POPE ST. JOHN PAUL II

Religion in general, and not just Catholicism or Christianity, often produces art for the simple reason that both religion and art are places where humanity explores its deepest questions. Just because we can identify several key features of a Catholic worldview that foster great literature does not mean that other worldviews do not produce great literature as well. Of course, they do! Moreover, in this book we have been careful to notice that worldviews that are not typically identified as "religious" often function as religion does, and so we should not be surprised to find art expressive of these worldviews as well. And, in as much as this art succeeds in portraying truth, goodness, and beauty, it is good art no matter the worldview of the artist.

Humans seek truth instinctually, and they often find it. Of course, humans also make mistakes, and the truth they perceive is often mixed with error. A Catholic engagement with art and literature from other worldviews is alert to both dynamics. Catholics are happy to take truth wherever we can find it. And we confidently expect to find it outside the bounds of the Church. But we are also aware of the impact of sin on the human person's search for truth and the real possibility of confusion and falsehood, not least in our own lives. And so, we approach all literature hoping to find the good, the true, and the beautiful, but we are not surprised to find, as in any human striving for truth, elements worthy of critique. Indeed, any honest search for truth is instructive even when it does not fully succeed.

The early Church Father Justin Martyr spoke of *logos spermatikos,* "seeds of the word," present in human culture. That is, the truths discerned by various human cultures contain, in seed form — undeveloped, perhaps, but real and oriented to growth and maturity — the truth of the Gospel. While it is often quoted with reference to faith and science, the maxim "truth does not contradict truth" applies to human culture as well. Works of art or literature that attend to reality perceptively have something to teach us all. That such works may flow from religious or secular worldviews that do not agree with Catholicism on every point does not change this fact. Throughout its history, Catholicism has been happy to learn from other worldviews, whether that be ancient philosophy for the Fathers of the Church, Aristotle in the Middle Ages, or the findings of contemporary science today. This does not mean overruling or replacing the truths of our faith, but enriching them and seeing their connection and application in ever wider circles. In fact, the more deeply rooted we become in an integrated Catholic worldview, the more capable we become of discerning the truth, beauty, and goodness in the world outside the Church.

WHAT IS LANGUAGE FOR?

We are not rid of God because we still have faith in grammar.

FRIEDRICH NIETZSCHE

We have already had the opportunity, in this chapter, to reflect on several important elements of a Catholic attitude toward language. In particular, we have noted the Scriptural emphasis on the power of words with respect to both creation and Incarnation. And we have recognized that language has both incredible capacity and also limitations. Let us conclude this chapter, then, with a brief reflection on what language is for. In short, language is a gift from God given to us for the purpose of communicating truth.

Notice that this means that language is inherently communal. *Communication* requires persons in relationship; language both shapes and is shaped by communities. Strikingly, the doctrine of the Trinity says that God is relational. And this follows from the Gospel of John's image of Jesus as the "Word of God." If God can *speak*, even before creation, then in God himself there is something relational. If language is an appropriate metaphor for thinking about the inner reality of God, then God is, somehow, communal.

Further, language is expressive of the self. Language is how we make ourselves known to one another. Trinitarian theology teaches that, in the case of God, this self-expression is so perfect that the expression itself is God. "The Word was with God, and the Word was God" (Jn 1:1). In our case, such self-expression falls short of perfection. We can communicate true things about ourselves to one another, but never perfectly. There is always a gap, sometimes larger, sometimes smaller, between what we really hope to convey and what the other is able to understand. That is one reason we repeat ourselves so often! Nevertheless, used honestly and well, language really can communicate truth. When it does so, it also forges genuine community of common understanding and shared meaning.

Those who are suspicious of the existence of objective truth, or of the human capacity to know such truth, are at least being internally consistent when they argue that language is merely about power and manipulation. Without objective truth, this is precisely what language becomes. When there is no measure outside the self by which language might be judged, when truth is bracketed or denied, the only measure left is power. In such a world, it is hard to deny that the one who can best use language to get what she desires can and should do so. If we are frustrated at the way language is used to control and manipulate people in advertising or politics or social media, we recognize this basic problem. Truth is often replaced by power as the ultimate criterion for the use of language.

This was foreseen by the great atheist philosopher Friedrich Nietzsche at the very beginning of what was to become postmodernism. Catholics can acknowledge that Nietzsche was right that, once truth is dispensed with, power is all that remains. We must disagree, however, with his judgment that it is the task of the strong to pursue power without reference to any truth beyond the self. But Nietzsche himself recognized that this is a virtually impossible task. This is the background to his famous aphorism, quoted at the beginning of this section, that we are not rid of God because we still believe in grammar. For Nietzsche, God is a limit on humanity's capacity. We cannot reach our human potential as long as there is something beyond us to which we are responsible. Rather, we must assert ourselves completely, making our own selves and our own world without any external limits.

But this is just what grammar represents! Grammar is a limit on our speech. It says that we must conform ourselves to commonly accepted rules in order to be understood. Without the rules of grammar, we can say whatever words we choose, in any order we like, but we will only be making noise; we will not be communicating. Grammar, then, is a great illustration of the fact that rules are not the opposite of freedom but the prerequisites of freedom. To speak only gibberish, unhindered by grammar, may look like freedom to those who think freedom means only lack of constraint. But it will not feel like freedom to the person who tries to communicate in this way. She will, instead, feel trapped and limited. But if freedom is ordered toward some end, if it means the capacity to achieve certain goals — to do good, to create beauty, to speak truth — then constraints are good and necessary. God and grammar are both external to us, making real demands on us. Such demands do not make us slaves; they make us free.

Lesson Plan Idea: Grammar

Grammar is rarely a student favorite in English class. It can feel confusing, arbitrary, and unnecessary. Before beginning a unit on grammar, it might be valuable to devise a lesson emphasizing the value of grammar in everyday communication. Everyone desires to be understood. Begin class by exploring some humorous misunderstandings, before discussing more serious and consequential misunderstandings. Students can share their own examples as well. The grammatical element need not be immediately emphasized, but eventually the role of grammar in preventing misunderstanding can be introduced through examples.

Discuss the role of grammar in human life and social interaction, and reflect on what life might be like without grammar. Finally, introduce the notion of grammar as an external rule that frees rather than enslaves, and the analogy with God. Discuss Nietzsche's famous quote. Consider prominently displaying the quote in the classroom throughout the unit and beyond. Keeping the quote on permanent display, so that students see it long before this particular lesson plan, might be a very effective way to build anticipation for the subject.

KEY TAKEAWAYS

Words and language are essential parts of what makes us human. That they are instances of the immaterial becoming material highlights the relationship between the spiritual and bodily aspects of our nature.

There is plenty of Catholic content to add to our Language Arts classes, and our students need to know their own Catholic literary heritage. But Catholic Academic Integration is not content to rest with this.

Catholicism teaches many things — about the Bible, creation, the Incarnation, the sacraments, and the human person — that lead to great literature.

Catholics expect to find truth, goodness, and beauty outside the visible bounds of the Church and confidently approach non-Catholic literature looking for them.

Grammar is a constraint that makes us more free and so is a great analogy for thinking about God's role in creation and human life.

Chapter 6
History

History might seem like a straightforward candidate for curriculum permeation. There is, after all, plenty of Catholic history to be studied, even in public schools. (There was no Catholic school in the small town where I grew up, but one of my most memorable school projects was a mock trial of Martin Luther in my Grade 9 history class.) A Catholic school can certainly be expected to put a little more focus on the Church in its study of history than other schools might, as we will explore below. But just studying more Catholic history is not enough. In addition to adding some Catholic *content*, we need to learn to see and to teach history from a Catholic point of view. We need to understand history in a Catholic *context*.

COUNTERING ANTI-CATHOLIC HISTORY

Consider, for instance, the problem of anti-Catholic bias built into many popular versions of history. Catholic history teachers should be able to critically engage with the standard narratives we encounter in areas such as the relationships between religion and violence or between the Church and science, or the development of the teaching of the Church on questions such as slavery. We should not, of course, whitewash the failings of the institutional Church or of its members. But we do need to show that much of what we hear in popular discourse about things like the Crusades, the Inquisition, or the Galileo affair is at least one-sided and often simply false.

How many Catholics know, for instance, that none of Galileo's "proofs" that the earth orbits the sun actually work? Or that the early modern witch trials were generally much worse in non-Catholic countries? Or that the Church never believed or taught that the earth was flat? This last notion, which many of us don't even think to question, was actually invented in the nineteenth century as anti-Catholic propaganda. (If these claims surprise you, go ahead and look them up. Wikipedia is actually quite reliable on these matters.) Sometimes, in an earnest desire to face up to our own flawed history with honesty and integrity, we even unwittingly perpetuate anti-Catholic propaganda in our own schools! Avoiding this would seem to be a bare minimum requirement in Catholic education.

Catholic teachers also need to be aware of the basic worldview that often underlies the one-sided and anti-Catholic interpretations of certain controversial episodes in the popular imagination. A key element of this worldview is "the myth of progress," and we will look into this in more detail below. For now, notice that one of the basic conceits of the modern world is that whatever comes later is almost certainly better. We imagine ancient people to be backwards and benighted. We use the adjective "medieval" to describe anything horrific or brutal, even if those horrific and brutal things happened in living memory (how odd that we call quintessentially modern things like concentration camps, genocides, and nuclear bombs "medieval"). When asked why they support certain ideas, people often say things like "Because it's 2015," as if that makes anything more or less true than it was in 2014 or 1776. And we often don't notice that these things are odd until they are pointed out to us. "The myth of progress" is a pair of glasses through which most contemporary people, including most Catholics, see the world.

Within this worldview, Catholicism is identified with the past and serves as a symbol of outdated ideas and beliefs that are best left behind. As such, it can become more important to use something like the history of the Crusades, for example, to present the Church in a certain light — ignorant, violent, imperialist — than to present a truthful and balanced account of the matter. But we should be able to grant that the Crusaders committed unjustifiable atrocities and still recognize that it is inconsistent to imagine that it was fine for Muslim armies to conquer Byzantium, but evil and imperialistic for Christian ones to try to liberate it.

And the utterly false notion that the Church had insisted the earth was flat until Columbus proved otherwise is brought into service any time someone wants to argue that some Catholic teaching or other needs "updating." The myth of progress is in the background of almost all contemporary anti-Catholic mythology. When we understand that basic context, we will be much better placed to recognize and to teach more reliable content, even, or perhaps especially, if elements of anti-Catholic mythology have entered standard reference works and textbooks.

In addition to addressing anti-Catholic bias in popular versions of history and learning to recognize the basic worldview behind these tellings of history, Catholic teachers should also be aware, as we explored at the beginning of Part II, that *the idea of history* is itself a product of Judeo-Christian revelation. It is only because the Bible tells us about *salvation history*, God's plan to save human beings from sin and bring creation to glorious fulfillment, that we have come to think of history itself in the way that we do. We might imagine that history is simply the recording (and perhaps analyzing) of past events, but it is much more than that. It is a whole way of interpreting the meaning of events that shapes how we think about them. Humans have had other ways of relating to and understanding the sequence of events in time and even of the idea of time itself. In the last section of this chapter, we will look at two of these: mythology and fate. Our consideration of these will highlight just how unique, and ultimately how biblical, the notion of history actually is and what difference that makes.

ADDING CATHOLIC CONTENT

Just as we would expect any school founded and operated by a given community to put a particular focus on that community's own history and its role in the broader history of the world, it is perfectly legitimate for a Catholic school to do the same. And so, in addition to the usual places where the Church shows up in standard curricula, we can be more attentive to the role of Catholicism in other times and places as well. For example, everyone studies the Church when they study the Crusades or the Reformation, but perhaps not when they study the Industrial Revolution. But Catholics should know about how Catholic Social Teaching developed precisely in response to the conditions of working people and to various ideological currents brought about by the Industrial Revolution. And if the Church features at all in a study of the Age of Exploration, it is often as one more colonialist European institution. Yet Catholics, at least, should know how the work of missionaries was often in conflict with the work of the colonizers, as is demonstrated in the stories of figures like Bartolomé de las Casas or St. Martin de Porres. Enslaving and exploiting people, it turns out, is rather incompatible with evangelizing them, and those committed to one of these were often opposed to the other.

Indeed, an introduction of the stories of the saints into history class can be a very effective way to add Catholic content. For the saints have lived in a vast array of historical contexts, and their stories often intersect with the major historical questions at play in illuminating ways. Think of Pope John Paul II at the end of the Cold War. Or Pope Gregory at the end of the Roman Empire. Think of Francis Xavier in the drama of the sixteenth-century contacts between Europeans and the great and ancient cultures of the East. Think of Juan Diego and Kateri Tekakwitha in North America. Or of Edith Stein and Franz Jägerstätter in Nazi Germany. Or of Katharine Drexel and Frances Cabrini in the United States. Or Catherine of Siena during the Avignon papacy. Or Oscar Romero in El Salvador. Or Paul Miki in sixteenth-century Japan and Charles Lwanga in nineteenth-century Uganda and Mark Ti Jianxiang during China's Boxer Rebellion.

The list could go on. In each case, the story of the saint serves to illuminate essential elements of the historical situation. Biography is a very valuable tool in the teaching of history, and we have beautiful, inspiring, and instructive biographies of Catholics from many of the times and places we study. In addition, saints' biographies have the advantage of being easily adaptable for use at any age. And it is a plain fact of Christian history that many saints' biographies include the reading of other saints' biographies. If we want to encourage a love of God and the pursuit of holiness, it is hard to find better content than the stories of the saints.

THE MYTH OF PROGRESS

Like every society, our contemporary modern society has its own creation story. For most of human history, this story goes, humans were ignorant and superstitious, beholden to crude and irrational religious beliefs because they did not have the knowledge or sophistication to make sense of the world the way we can today. Then, in early modern Europe, humanity started throwing off these shackles, first through the Reformation and its rejection of Church authority, and then, in rapid succession, through the Scientific Revolution and the Enlightenment, which together banished superstition and set humanity on the path to reason, peace, and prosperity. Any bumps on that road are attributed to the vestiges of the older worldviews that still need to be eliminated, and never to the new ways of thinking themselves.

That, at least, is the "modern" view. Postmodernism, as we saw in chapter 2, is willing to critique these "new" ways of thinking — if not always in exactly the same ways a Catholic might — and emerged precisely when the carnage of the twentieth century made this "modern" view less and less defensible. That the most "advanced" nations in human history were also those capable of such inhuman destruction led people to question the story modernity told about itself. But, despite postmodernism's remarkable influence in contemporary society, elements of the modern worldview remain common, even dominant, in areas such as the popular understanding of history. The "myth of progress" is a prime example.

Familiar narratives about witch hunts and crusades and a flat earth and "poor Galileo" work just as myths are supposed to. The ritual retelling of these stories makes sense of the world from a particular point of view and reaffirms the identities and beliefs of those who tell and hear them. Those telling the stories generally don't ask what it means for their worldview that the Church never taught the earth was flat or that Galileo himself — for all his troubles — never wavered in the Catholic faith that the telling of his story is supposed to subvert. The myths are told in such a way as to obscure such inconvenient facts and discourage any awkward questions.

WAS RELIGION INVENTED TO CONTROL THE MASSES?

The whole of the Hebrew Bible is a polemic against power.

RABBI JONATHAN SACKS

To understand this dynamic better, let us look in a little more depth at just one standard element of the myth of progress: the notion that religion was invented by social elites in order to keep the ignorant multitudes in their thrall. Karl Marx famously called religion "the opiate of the masses." Interestingly enough, this critique is not all that original to Marx. Several Church Fathers made similar critiques of the pagan religions on offer in ancient Rome. In his great work *The City of God*, for instance, Saint Augustine was particularly concerned about religion that sacralized politics, something of which Marxism is not wholly innocent. So yes, religions and ideologies can certainly be invented or employed by elites to keep the downtrodden in their place. Christianity wouldn't dream of denying it. Moreover, Christians should always be wary of the temptation to align too closely with political power for just this reason. Politics is always happy to co-opt religion for its own ends.

But where did this insight come from in the first place? The Bible! The Old Testament is the story of a nation of nobodies formed from a group of escaped slaves. Unlike much of the mythological propaganda promulgated to justify and buttress the power structures of Israel's neighbors, Scripture is a story of how power corrupts and how the oppression of the weak by the strong is abhorrent in the eyes of God. From this point of view, one of the worst things Israel does in the whole Old Testament is to demand a king "like other nations" (1 Sm 8:5). God was the only possible just king. Any human king, Israel was prophetically warned, would exploit and abuse them.

Indeed, in the Bible, you can generally spot a false prophet because he is willing to say what pleases those in power. The true prophets, on the other hand, are regularly in danger from those in power who do not like what they have to say. This pattern, not incidentally, is precisely what plays out in the life of Jesus.

In other words, it might well be the case that *some religions were* invented to keep power with the powerful. And it is certainly the case that religion in general, including Christianity itself, *can* be used this way. But it is precisely the Judeo-Christian view presented in Scripture that most powerfully critiques such abuse. Any Christians misusing their religion in this way are cutting off the very branch on which they sit. Consider how delightfully ironic it is that African American slaves were unintentionally taught by their unwitting oppressors that the God of the Bible is on the side not of the masters, but of the slaves themselves, and that he desires — even works for, even promises — their liberation!

It is no coincidence that political ideologies are at least as vulnerable as any religion to the criticism of being designed to subjugate the masses. One of the key features of the modern creation story is the scapegoating of religion so that modern people are oblivious to the fact that other actors — nation states, corporations, ideologies — are at least as bad as religion is supposed to be. Such scapegoating depends to a large degree on the widely held notion that religion is somehow uniquely prone to violence. But is this notion true?

"THE MYTH OF RELIGIOUS VIOLENCE"

Religion is the cause of most wars in the world.

EVERY SECOND PERSON YOU MEET

In *The Myth of Religious Violence*, Catholic theologian William T. Cavanaugh demonstrates how the so-called wars of religion in sixteenth-century Europe were not really wars of religion at all. Those conflicts are, in fact, better understood as the founding violence of the modern European nation states. Cavanaugh shows in remarkable detail how religious affiliation was, in fact, a very poor predictor of who would fight whom during this series of conflicts, and that matters of politics and statecraft trumped concerns about religious truth again and again.

The story that was told about the "wars of religion," however, including the name they were given, serves an essential function in the modern creation story. If those bloody conflicts could be blamed on religion, then the modern nation states of Europe could be presented as the solution to religious violence. Supposedly violent religion would then be relegated to the private sphere, where it is more easily managed. The real business of the world, which of course includes a monopoly on violence, would now be seen to by the nation states whose violence, we are assured, would always be rational and justified.

It is, of course, difficult to imagine any institution in history responsible for more bloodshed than the modern nation state in its various iterations, both in Europe and wherever it has been exported around the world. But somehow it is a truism in our society that religion is the cause of most of the world's wars. The myth of religious violence is not only used to slander religion; it is used to blind us to the reality of the violence employed by "rational" secular forces. In a Catholic history class, we should certainly demonstrate that it is false that religion is uniquely violent; but we should also teach students to recognize the real violence we overlook when religion is made to play the villain.

"THE RIGHT SIDE OF HISTORY"

One of the more dangerous consequences of the myth of progress is the idea that being on a given side of a contentious social issue puts one "on the right side of history." If the present is always better than the past and the future will be better than the present, then anyone advocating for radical societal change can harness the myth of progress as a rhetorical tool. To ask critical questions about radical proposals is to "obstruct progress." And to oppose any such proposals is to be "on the wrong side of history."

In the worst cases, this is used to justify violence against ideological opponents. Communism is explicit on this point: history is irrevocably going in a certain direction, and violence is justified to help it get there. The death toll of various communist revolutions and governments is almost unfathomable. But communism is far from the only bad idea that imagined itself to be on the right side of history.

In the early twentieth century, the eugenics movement — the idea that those humans "less fit" to reproduce should be eliminated from the gene pool — was widely accepted in progressive circles. It certainly seemed to be on the right side of history, and those opposed — including, notably, the Catholic Church — were derided as anti-progress. The eugenics movement led to things like forced sterilizations, and its legacy includes the continued targeting of racial minorities by abortion providers like Planned Parenthood.

Canada's shameful history of residential schools — where First Nations children were often forcibly removed from their families before being stripped of their language and culture, to say nothing of the endemic abuse in many of these institutions — was also imagined by its advocates to be part of moving history in the right direction. This time, instead of denouncing the evil, the Catholic Church and other Christian churches in Canada cooperated with the government of Canada in running the schools. This remains a source of both shame and of strained relations between First Nations people and the churches to this day. Many First Nations children died from neglect, abuse, or disease in Canada's residential schools, and the system's legacy includes generational trauma in families of survivors that persists long after the schools have closed their doors.

It is sobering to consider how easy it is for people to justify such staggering human costs when they are convinced that their cause is "on the right side of history."

HISTORY AS A JUDEO-CHRISTIAN IDEA

The word *myth* is often used to mean two different things. First, it can mean "falsehood." This is how we use it, for instance, when we say that it is a "myth" that the medieval Church taught that the earth is flat or that vaccines cause autism. Second, it can refer to a genre of literature or kind of storytelling, like that found in the first chapters of the Book of Genesis. Every culture tells stories in order to ponder life's biggest questions, to understand its own identity, and to orient its people to live according to its values. This is the function of mythology. Paradoxically, while we sometimes use the word *myth* to mean simply "falsehood," myth, in this second sense, is how cultures communicate that which they believe to be most true.

To make matters more confusing, it is possible to use the term *myth* to mean both of these things at the same time. That, in fact, is precisely what I was doing in the last section. The myth of progress is both an example of mythology — a kind of storytelling to shape a culture's identity and values — and a whole collection of falsehoods. But notice that the myth of progress does not present itself as myth, but as history. The Book of Genesis lets us know, by the presence of a talking snake, for example, when we are in the realm of mythology and that the story we are reading should be interpreted as making truth claims about things like identity (e.g., human beings are made in God's image) and value (e.g., creation is good and intended and loved by God), not about history (e.g., the age of the earth). The myth of progress gives us no such overt clues. In fact, for modern mythology to work, it needs to portray itself *as history* because part of modern mythology is that modernity has moved beyond mythology!

Like its modern successors, much ancient mythology was also designed to cover up or disguise elements of reality. In fact, the words *myth* and *mute* come from the same Greek root; the Greeks were aware of this function of myth. In particular, both ancient and modern mythologies are typically used to justify and support a given political order. Contrast this with Judeo-Christian revelation, which denounces the exploitative political orders, not only of Israel's neighbors, but even of Israel itself! The ability to be self-critical is generally a very good sign of authenticity, and the Old Testament has this in spades. To take just one prominent example, both Cain (in the Old Testament) and Romulus (in Roman mythology) kill their brothers and go on to found cities. But Roman mythology justifies Romulus's killing of Remus and hails him as the father of the city. The Bible, on the other hand, sides with Abel.

PROPAGANDA

Cultures do manage, of course, to also say true things in their mythologies. While sin does cloud our judgment, humans are made for truth, and those who seek it honestly tend not to come up empty-handed. The Bible and the Church both explicitly teach that truth is accessible to human persons and cultures outside of Divine Revelation. So, we should expect genuine human wisdom to be present in the mythologies of the world, even in modern myths. (Part of modern mythology is the wonder of science, and science actually *is* pretty great!) And so, it is quite justifiable that we classify both the first chapters of Genesis and the kinds of stories all cultures tell about themselves as mythology.

On the other hand, perhaps we need another category for thinking about those elements of mythology that are told to disguise reality, to avoid critique, and to justify an unjust social order. Fortunately, we have an excellent word in English for just such elements: propaganda. History, then, need not be opposed to myth in general. The early chapters of Genesis are not in competition with history; they are just doing different work than history. They are interested in eternal truths about God, creation, and humanity, not about temporal events, chronologies, or locales. But history, at least as we heirs of the biblical worldview have come to understand it, *is* opposed to propaganda.

It is said, with some truth, that the winners write the history books. But it is our biblical heritage that makes us suspect that this is not necessarily a good thing. Because the Bible was not written by the winners, but by the losers. The Old Testament is a story of a weak and insignificant nation caught up in the histories of great empires: conquered, enslaved, deported, divided, cut down to a stump. The New Testament, for its part, begins with the story of an occupied territory ("In those days a decree went out from Emperor Augustus ..." [Lk 2:1]) and an unjust execution of an innocent resident of that territory by the occupying empire's arbitrary and self-serving power. Many of the men who wrote it were executed by that same empire. In both the Old and New Testaments, God is on the side of the losers!

Parts of the Bible are what we might call history, and parts of it are not. But the very idea that the story of the world is not identical to the story that the powerful tell in order to justify their power is biblical to the core. Parts of the Bible are what we might call myth, and parts of it are not. But it is the Bible that gives us the tools to distinguish between stories that human cultures tell to convey their best wisdom about life and stories that are devised to keep us from asking too many questions. History, as we understand it, means that the perspective of the world's victims is more important than the perspective of the world's victors. Historical writing often fails to live up to this standard, but it is the existence of the standard itself that proves the point. Because of the Bible, history is the opposite of propaganda.

FATE

One of the great stories of Greek mythology is that of King Oedipus. Oedipus is told that he will kill his father and marry his mother. To avoid this terrible fate, Oedipus flees far away but, through a series of misadventures, it is precisely the actions he takes to avoid killing his father and marrying his mother that lead him to do just that. In Greek mythology, fate is even more powerful than the gods. What is going on here?

When we think about it, it is not hard to imagine why humans would tell stories like this. Life is hard. And we often feel powerless in the face of overwhelming realities that are far beyond us. It really can feel as if nothing we do can make any real difference. The ancient Greeks are not the only ones to tell stories like this. They can be found in other cultures, including our own. One form they take in modern society is the pseudo-scientific denial of free will. The feeling of choice, we are told, is an illusion, an epiphenomenon of the brain. Other cultures have questioned or denied free will, but ours does so using the language and categories of science. But whether we are ancient Greeks or modern westerners, the moral of the story is the same. Nothing really matters in the end. Whatever will be will be. You can't make a difference.

Such fatalism is often accompanied by a cyclical notion of history. Many cultures have asserted that whatever is happening has happened before and will happen again. In such a worldview, nothing ever *really* changes. It is against this backdrop that we can understand how Israel's story of God's actions in history was so revolutionary. Humanity had generally considered the gods to be part of the world system. This is why the Greeks could believe that fate was even stronger than the gods. But Israel's transcendent Creator God was not bound in this way. Israel understood that there was an irreducible difference between Creator and creation, that God was outside the system, so to speak, and that, consequently, God was transcendentally free with respect to creation. Only such a god as this God could genuinely alter the course of history. This is why one of the gifts that the Bible gives to humanity is the concept of linear time. If God can genuinely intervene and change the course of history, there can be no infinitely repeating cycles. History is open-ended. And what is more, human actions make a real difference. History, at least as it has been understood in Judeo-Christian cultures, is not merely the chronicling of events. It is, rather, the very opposite of fate.*

---

* On this point, I cannot recommend highly enough Margaret Visser's 2002 Massey Lectures, "Beyond Fate." Originally delivered as lectures, you can listen to them online, or read them in book form.

PROVIDENCE, FREE WILL, AND OUR PARTICIPATION IN THE SALVATION OF THE WORLD

Christians believe two things: God is in charge of history *and* human freedom is real and makes a genuine difference. These two things might seem tricky to reconcile at first glance. It is God's transcendence that makes this possible. If God's freedom were in competition with human freedom, then either God's will could be done or humans could be free, but not both. But because God's freedom transcends, even grounds, human freedom, God's providence and human freedom can coexist. Indeed, God wills that humans be free, and so we are.

We can get a glimpse of this reality when we look at human dynamics. Parents of small children learn very quickly that if they get in a battle of wills, they are often in for a long night. Generally speaking, no one wins these battles. Even if someone — be it parent or child — eventually caves in, everyone feels worse afterwards. And no one feels more free. But when parents are at their most creative and their most free, they often find that they can best handle the situation not by opposing the child's freedom with their own, but by engaging it. For example, when a child says something that isn't true, it is generally more effective to ask curious and gently critical questions about their claim than to immediately scold them for lying. This is true of all other human relationships as well. With adults we might speak of allowing someone to "save face." Giving such an opportunity requires creativity. When conflict is brewing, the person with the most freedom in the moment can often engage the freedom of others to seek a resolution where everyone feels free at the end.

The basic rule is this: The person with the most freedom can transcend and ground the freedom of the person with less freedom. Because God is completely free — infinitely more free than even the best human parents — God can always engage us in our freedom without coercion. So, in fact, it is not when we are most free that God's will confronts us as an obstacle, but when we are least free. This is clear, for instance, to anyone who has ever struggled with addiction.

All of which is to say that history, from a Christian point of view, is the arena for the glorious interplay of divine and human freedom. Because God is free and has intervened in history, human life matters. We can achieve genuine good, and we can do real harm. We cannot overrule God's plan for the salvation of the world, but we can participate in it or reject it in ways that have real and lasting consequences. History as a category is possible because of the biblical notion of a transcendent Creator God. And what it means for you and your students is that your life and your choices really matter.

Assignment Idea: Lives of the Saints

For any historical period you are studying, have students do presentations on lives of saints for their classmates. Have them pay particular attention to historical context and how that context explains features of the saint's life. For example, Edith Stein was a Jewish woman in Nazi Germany. Mark Ti Jianxiag was an opium addict at a time when British merchants were cultivating opium addiction among the Chinese. Pope John Paul II's native Poland was a satellite state of the USSR during the Cold War. Elizabeth Ann Seton was a Catholic convert from a prominent Protestant family in the nineteenth-century United States, where Protestantism was much more socially respectable than Catholicism. If, over the course of a semester or year, each student were to study and present on one saint, the students would learn a lot of history, be introduced to twenty to thirty saints, and perhaps form a lifelong friendship with a favorite saint. Indeed, Catherine of Siena has been in my corner ever since an undergraduate history paper I wrote on medieval women mystics.

KEY TAKEAWAYS

Several standard historical narratives contain anti-Catholic propaganda. At minimum, we must strive not to perpetuate this in Catholic schools.

In a Catholic school, attention can be brought to the Church's role in many historical episodes that are not typically associated with Church. The lives of the saints can be a great way to approach this.

Much of modernity's self-understanding is rooted in a telling of history that is more mythological than historical. In a Catholic school, we need to be able to recognize and critique this approach to history.

It is the Bible that first teaches us that real history is not the stories the powerful tell to justify their social positions, — that is, propaganda — but must always include the voices of the oppressed.

It is the Bible's vision of a transcendent God that makes history as we understand it — open-ended, responsive to genuine freedom — possible. And this means you, your life, and your choices actually matter.

Chapter 7
Math

If there is one subject that people instinctively imagine cannot be taught from a Catholic point of view, it is math. At the level of content, this is mostly true. There are no formulas or equations that change because the person employing them believes in the Resurrection. I say mostly, however, because there are some things you might teach in math class, like biographical details of great mathematicians or the historical development of different branches of mathematics, that can have some more specifically faith-based content.

Did you know, for example, that a whole branch of contemporary mathematics — actuarial science — was developed because of the biblical injunction to care for the widow and the orphan? Actuarial science is the math used by insurance companies to figure out what rates they need to charge to be able to provide different levels of coverage. And it was first developed by Presbyterians who were trying to figure out how to best provide for the widows and orphans left behind when their clergymen husbands and fathers passed away. The foundation of the Knights of Columbus — a Catholic fraternal benefit society with a great insurance program — had a similar impetus: caring for the widows and orphans left behind when men died young through dangerous occupations or other misfortunes.

And while this example is very specifically Christian — a Christian denomination developing a branch of mathematics to do something they felt called by the Bible to do — it is also part of a broader conversation to be had about math and ethics. However "neutral" the content of math may seem in itself, when we get to the question of *how to use math*, such neutrality disappears. Math can be used to care for widows and orphans, but it can also be used to cook books or embezzle or defraud. Statistics can be manipulated in order to confuse and obfuscate by mainstream media and conspiracy theorists alike. Or honest fact checkers can use them to help us better understand the truth. Humanity's notoriously bad grasp of probability leaves us open to manipulation by conspiracists and casinos. At the same time, our incredible achievements in math mean we can build truly wondrous things like railway bridges and rocket ships and retirement plans. Using math, we *can* do all kinds of amazing things. That kind of power should always lead us to ask what we *should* do.

But it is fair to say that all these things — biography, history, ethics — no matter how interesting and valuable they are and how connected with math they might be, are not themselves math. And it is math itself that concerns us here. It is easy to focus our attention on what math can do and overlook what math *means*. Many of us have never really thought, for example, about what it means that math actually works. Or that human beings can do math. Because math works as such a valuable tool for studying creation, it certainly tells us something about the Creator. And the fact that *we humans* do math — we don't know any other creature that does — says something about us as well. Finally, Catholicism is interested in everything because God created everything and saw that it was good. Math is a unique and privileged way of perceiving the truth, goodness, and beauty of God's creation. It is, therefore, a path to God himself.

AN INTELLIGIBLE CREATION

Can you remember a moment when you were overwhelmed by the beauty or coherence of creation? Or a time when you were simply stunned by an acute awareness that something exists, rather than nothing? The smallest things can trip this kind of liminal experience in us, things like holding a baby, or peacefully contemplating some tiny, exquisite element of nature, like an ant on a leaf. Or solving a math problem! What these things, and many others you could list, have in common is that they are particularly intense encounters with the truth, goodness, and beauty in creation, and they witness to the transcendent truth, goodness, and beauty of God, the Creator.

Perhaps the most remarkable, awe-inspiring thing about math is that it works! That is to say, we humans manage to a) observe reality; b) construct a purely abstract system from our experience of it; c) work with the elements of that system — in ways that are simultaneously rational, complex, beautiful, and often genuinely surprising — to find out true things about reality we could never have discerned by mere observation; and then, d) often enough, use what we have learned to shape that reality. We easily take all this for granted, but it should blow our minds!

And there are several implications of this that demand our attention. For starters, notice that the universe is, at the same time, both deeply mysterious and deeply intelligible. The challenge of the mathematician is not that the world does not make sense, but that it makes so much sense. After thousands of years, we do not feel that we are approaching the end of what math can do, but that we are only beginning to see its potential for exploring the mystery of creation.

Indeed, there is an analogy between math and creation, on the one hand, and theology and the Creator, on the other. In both cases, the mystery under study seems to grow rather than shrink as it is explored. In math, an image of God's infinity is built into creation. The more we know, the more we can know and the more we recognize just how much more remains to be learned. As math reveals truths about creation, it simultaneously reveals truths about God. For only a God that is both rational and surprising, simultaneously deeply coherent and deeply mysterious, could create the reality that is disclosed to us by our study of math.

ENCOUNTERING TRUTH

While mysterious, the reality we perceive through math is not haphazard or capricious. It is orderly and intelligible. This means that there are true things about creation that we can both know and communicate to others. In contradiction to much contemporary thought, math teaches us that truth exists and that we have genuine access to it. More than that, math also teaches us about the joy to be found in pursuing and finding truth.

There is truth, of course, in subjects like history. But such truth typically comes to us secondhand. It must, in other words, be taken on faith. Now, taking certain kinds of things on faith, as we have seen in chapter 3, is a perfectly reasonable thing to do. On the other hand, there is also great value in the kind of knowledge that can be learned by direct experience of reality. In fact, those who ask us to take things on faith must refer to either their own firsthand knowledge or that of others whom they trust. So, acknowledging the value of faith does nothing to denigrate the value of direct experience. With math, students have a concrete, personal experience of finding and communicating truth first-hand. The value of such knowledge — truth that is its own evidence, that, once understood, cannot be denied — should not be underestimated. Why not?

Practical or applied mathematics is very valuable. Using math to do good is part of what it means to be stewards of creation. It is a kind of drawing out of the remarkable potentialities God has built into creation. But there is also pure or theoretical mathematics, where mathematicians study without any practical end in mind except to learn true things. Some of these things end up having unforeseen practical applications, but that is not the central point. In math, as in the rest of life, truth can and should be sought for its own sake. Catholicism teaches that humanity is made for truth. The true knowledge of the world that we learn through math, and the joy we find in learning such truth, confirm this conviction. A Catholic math class should be a place where students learn to rejoice in God's truth.

MATH IS SPIRITUAL

You have arranged all things by measure and number and weight.

WISDOM 11:20

Another implication of math and how it works is that math is a spiritual practice. This might sound odd. For while we can certainly approach math in a spiritual frame of mind, treating our work as the pursuit of God's truth written into creation, we know that such an explicit attitude is not necessary for math to work. The atheist can do math as well as the believer can. The deeper point is that, even when the atheist does math, he is doing something spiritual. To do math is to abstract from the material realm, seeking truth and meaning in ways that transcend physical creation. The search for truth and meaning is, by definition, spiritual work.

Catholicism insists that reality is more than just physical reality — indeed, that spiritual realities are, in a sense, more real than physical ones. God and angels and human souls are such spiritual realities; so are ideals like justice or freedom. Even things like nation states or money cannot be reduced to their physical elements but, precisely in order to be the kinds of things that they are, must be infused with spirit, with meaning. How else could coins and bills become simply numbers in an account? Numbers and equations and formulas are also nonphysical things that are, nonetheless, real.

Let's pause for a moment to ask what we mean by "real" in this case. Too often, contemporary people use the word *real* as a synonym for *physical*. This leads to all kinds of confusion, as when, for example, we try to explain the Catholic belief that Christ is *really* present in the Eucharist. Folks easily imagine that such a "real" presence should be discernible using something like a microscope or even a mass spectrometer. Atheists have even kidnapped consecrated hosts and taken them to the lab, triumphantly announcing that they have proved Catholic teaching false when their instruments can discern only bread. But the doctrine of transubstantiation expects just that result! It explicitly says that those aspects of reality which are detectible to the senses, even the senses aided by very precise scientific instruments — what it calls "accidents" — do not change at all at the consecration. What the Church considers most "real" is not the physical elements of bread and wine, but an even deeper reality — what the doctrine calls "substance" — that transcends those physical elements, holds them together in an intelligible unity, and makes them to be what they are. This deeper reality exists at the level of spirit; that is, at the level of meaning and identity. And so, God, being the author of creation and the giver of meaning and identity, can miraculously change bread and wine into the Body and Blood of Christ without changing their physical makeup one whit.*

To a nonbeliever, this appeal to some reality deeper than the physical to explain the Catholic belief in Christ's real presence in the Eucharist will certainly look like a stretch. But it is hard to find a better illustration that reality is deeper than the merely physical — that reality includes *meaning* — than math! Math does not impose meaning on a meaningless physical reality so that we can manipulate that reality to our own ends. Reality strenuously resists any such imposition. Rather, math works by discerning the meaning inherent in reality and working with it *as it is*.

Some immaterial thing like "three-ness," for example, is not something we could make up, but only something we could discover by honest observation. Three-ness is real. And though it is seen or expressed in physical reality, it cannot ever be pointed to as its own independent physical thing. In this it is somewhat analogous to the human soul. We can never point to a soul or find it in a lab. But we *can* tell the difference between a living body and a corpse. We can never point to a three, either. But we can know how many apples are left if we start with four and eat one. Math is about the intelligibility of physical reality, intelligibility that is only accessible to an intellect that can discern truth from falsehood. These are spiritual operations. Math teaches us

---

*We can leave aside the question of Eucharistic miracles here. They are the exception, not the rule. And not even the most fervent believer in such miracles thinks that there must be physically discernible changes in the elements for a consecration to be valid.

that reality cannot be reduced to the physical.

MATH AND VIRTUE

Recall that a Catholic education is not primarily about communicating true content, as essential as that is, but about forming students by cultivating virtue. A Catholic education is about formation, not just information. What role can math play in such formation?

In math, we encounter reality in a way that we cannot ignore or alter or reinterpret to mean something other than what it means. Such a recalcitrant reality works as a kind of whetstone against which we can sharpen both our minds and our souls. Consider the following analogy from chess. Unlike games that use cards or dice, chess is a game with no element of luck or chance. It is pure strategy. During games, competitive players record every move. At tournaments, opposing players often reconvene immediately after their game ends to go over it together. The just completed game is a kind of puzzle for them to solve as a team. If both players play perfectly, the game would end in a draw. So, by definition, if someone loses, it's because he made a mistake somewhere. The first task of this joint analysis is to find that one key mistake. There are generally many other mistakes to be found as well. Even the winners have generally made significant errors that, had they been caught in them, could have cost them the game.

The fascinating thing about this practice is that the players have nowhere to hide. The truth is right before them. Analyzing a chess match is a matter of looking assiduously for your mistakes, owning them, and learning from them. It is, in other words, a great exercise in virtues like diligence, honesty, and humility. The fact that it is often done with your opponent makes it even harder to hide from reality, because the kinds of things we are tempted to tell ourselves to justify our mistakes don't survive such a public airing very well. And working with an opponent also challenges players to develop virtues like clarity and charity in speech, careful listening, patience, and magnanimity.

The parallels with math are not hard to see. Imagine a student working through a problem at the board. He makes a mistake, but the wise teacher quickly and discreetly indicates that those students who recognize the error should hold their tongues. The student at the board eventually realizes there is a problem. What to do? Like the chess players, the student has a record of his every move. So, it is time to go back and look honestly for his mistake. If an answer is wrong or impossible, the mistake must be in there somewhere. There is no room for laziness or deception or pride here. The task demands diligence, honesty, and humility. And, of course, this kind of thing is often done in groups, with the attendant social virtues at the ready.

Now, imagine the teacher had simply stopped the student when he made the initial mistake. What would that have communicated? He had simply gotten the thing wrong. He had failed. What mattered was the right answer, and he wasn't going to get it. But letting the student keep working until his mistake became obvious to him and then having him seek, find, and correct that mistake on his own teaches much more than math. It teaches virtue. The Catholic teacher is always attentive to this element of education, and math provides a specific set of tools for just this task.

This is not to suggest that there are not virtue-building encounters with truth to be had in other subject areas. Of course there are! But the logical structure of the truth encountered in math is so clear and unambiguous that it is great for training the mind to recognize, know, and love truth. In fact, it is just this lack of ambiguity that leads some people to imagine that all truth can be reduced to mathematical truth or, conversely, that if something cannot be reduced to mathematical truth, then it is not true in any meaningful way. This kind of reductionism is self-refuting. The claim that all truth is mathematical is not a mathematical claim, nor can it be reduced to one without presuming what it purports to demonstrate. Nevertheless, math *is* a uniquely objective way of encountering reality.

This uniqueness does not make other ways somehow less valid. Rather, because creation is coherent and intelligible, math both lends its intelligibility to other ways of knowing, such as physics or some forms of philosophy, and develops intellectual virtues that are transferable to other ways of knowing. Consider our public discourse. What would happen, for instance, if we were to apply what we know about seeking the truth from math to a Facebook conversation that has gone off the rails? If a conversation has stopped working, could we go back in the thread and find the place where it got off track, fix that mistake, and start again from there?

The analogy is not perfect, of course. A Facebook conversation will include a variety of subjective factors that are not present in a math proof. For example, it is much harder to admit you made a mistake on Facebook where your personal identity or status in a group can feel at stake than in front of a math class where your error is simply undeniable and where everyone is on the same team. But, granted such differences, virtues like diligence, honesty, and humility will certainly help us on social media. Subjective factors might make it harder to be humble on Facebook than in math class, but virtue, like most things, takes practice in easier contexts before it can be skillfully deployed in more difficult ones.

MATH AND BEAUTY

Music is pleasure the human mind experiences from counting without being aware that it is counting.

ATTRIBUTED TO GOTTFRIED LEIBNIZ

We might be tempted to think of math and beauty as almost mutually exclusive categories. If beauty is in the eye of the beholder, if beauty is subjective, what can it have to do with math, which is so stubbornly objective? Math and art are easily imagined as being on opposite ends of an objective-subjective spectrum. On the other hand, most of us have had an experience of math as beautiful. There is something captivating about an elegant proof in Euclidean geometry, for instance, that seems to touch the same part of our souls as great art or beauty in nature. How shall we square this circle?

Math and art are opposites, in a way. But they might be more like two sides of a coin, expressing a unified truth through different forms. As we shall see in chapter 12, art is a kind of materializing of spiritual values. The artist expresses things like hope or despair, love or hate, faith or doubt, through things like ink on a page or carved stone or oil and canvas or vibrations in the air detected by your inner ear. Math goes in the other direction, moving from the material realm into the spiritual. It derives from careful observation of material reality, but then abstracts from that reality to say true things about it in a basically immaterial way. You can point to a bit of ink on paper that your culture has agreed means "three," but you can't ever point at a three. Art and math, then, are both rooted in reality as material and spiritual, and each is well suited to expressing true things about that reality, though their modes of communicating truth are shaped by their particular tasks.

What, then, of beauty's being in the eye of the beholder? As with most proverbs, there is certainly some truth to this. Every person's subjective experience of reality has been shaped in unique ways by personal experience, history, culture, even genetics. And so, the different forms beauty takes will impact individuals in unique ways. This does not mean beauty is simply arbitrary or purely subjective and unrelated to truth or goodness. It only means that few of us are well equipped to appreciate beauty in all its forms. Indeed, learning to appreciate beauty in places where you would not have thought to look for it is a most rewarding and humanizing experience. But such experience also implies that there is beauty in places where we have not yet learned to see it. In other words, beauty exists in reality *before* it exists in the eyes of the beholder.

This has at least two interesting connections with math. The first is that math is beautiful whether or not a given person has developed an appreciation for that beauty. One central task of the math teacher, then, is to highlight the beauty of mathematics. This need not be restricted to Catholic math teachers, by the way, though in a Catholic context, the relationship between the beauty of math and wonder at God's good creation can be brought out more explicitly. Catholic math teachers, starting in the earliest grades, should saturate their classes (and adorn their classrooms) with the language of wonder and beauty.

A second connection is to explore the role of math in things we find beautiful. Math is an abstraction from physical reality. This means that material things, like color or music, can be described and explored in mathematical terms. In fact, ancient and medieval curricula placed music within the quadrivium — alongside astronomy, geometry, and arithmetic — because it is so mathematical. Things like octaves, tones and semitones, and time signatures are all defined mathematically. And the wondrous thing is that we can actually look at the relationship between the mathematical structures of different pieces of music and how such pieces of music make us *feel*. The difference between a major and a minor scale can be described with math! In fact, we could even define singing, as opposed to normal speech, using math. Singing is, in fact, much more mathematically regular than normal speech. That is why we find it more beautiful and easier to remember.

Music might be the easiest arena in which to explore the connection between math and beauty, but the same can be done with elements of the plastic arts such as color or proportion. That different colors work well together, what interior designers might call a "palette," can be explored and described mathematically. The way to create the impression of depth in a sketch or painting can be explored and described mathematically. The ways in which symmetry or asymmetry or proportion (like the famous "Golden Ratio") create harmony and balance in painting or sculpture or photography can be explored and described mathematically. Not only is math beautiful in itself, but math gives us tools to explore and understand beauty in art. Because math is rooted in the intelligibility that underlies the whole of material creation, it can lend its own intelligibility not just to science and philosophy, but to art and the pursuit of beauty as well.

Lesson Plan Idea: Math and Music

Choose a selection of pieces of music that evoke different feelings and play them for the class. Have a discussion exploring how the different pieces made the students feel. Then lead the class in a mathematical exploration of the characteristics of the different pieces, watching for congruences between different characteristics and the emotional impact of the pieces. (Doing this cross-curricularly, with a music teacher who could bring in some basic music theory, would add real richness to the lesson.) Students could be brought to see, for example, how music in a minor key feels different than music in a major key and what that relationship looks like mathematically. As an assignment, ask students to choose a favorite piece of music (it would be ideal if the class was encouraged to make selections from a wide variety of genres) on which to do a similar kind of analysis and present it before the class. This could be done individually or as a group.

KEY TAKEAWAYS

While the content of math is, in a sense, neutral, the study of mathematical content cannot be separated from questions about the use of math and, especially, the meaning of math. These things are never neutral.

Math discloses to us the intelligibility and orderliness of creation and therefore tells us much about the Creator.

Because it seeks truth and meaning beyond the physical aspects of creation, math is spiritual work.

Math is an encounter with reality that should be an occasion for the development of virtue.

A Catholic math class will emphasize the beauty of math as part of the beauty of creation. Moreover, math can help us understand beauty in other contexts, like nature or the arts.

Chapter 8
Science

Catholic science teachers have one of the most important tasks in the evangelizing mission of the Church today. The notion that science and religion are enemies, incompatible ways of viewing the world, is very widespread in our contemporary culture. Study after study indicates that this misapprehension is an important factor for many young people who walk away from the Church. They have been given the impression that science makes religion obsolete, that questions that used to be answered by religion are now answered, and much more adequately, by science. It is not uncommon for young people, asked why they left the Church, to answer, "Because I believe in science."

Science teachers, you are on the front lines! If you teach in a Catholic school, it is part of your job to develop your own expertise, not only in science, but in the relationship between science and Catholic faith. If you do not cultivate your own Catholic worldview with respect to science, you will not be teaching your subject from a neutral point of view. Rather, the unquestioned presuppositions of the broader culture will find their way into your classroom unnoticed, through curricula and resources, through your students, even through your own blind spots. Those presuppositions can subtly undermine faith, no matter how loudly our Catholic schools insist, as they should, that faith and science are compatible. If, on the other hand, you take seriously your task of developing expertise in this area, your own life of faith will be enriched, as will your appreciation of the beauty of science. You will come to see not merely that faith and science can peacefully coexist, but even that, in some sense, they need one another. When you can teach from that conviction, science class becomes an encounter between you, your students, and the God who is present in all things.

The question of the relationship between science and Catholic faith is large and many-faceted. This chapter cannot hope to convey everything that a Catholic science teacher needs to know. But it should give you a good sense of the kinds of things Catholic science teachers need to be aware of and some starting points for thinking about those issues. It will also provide some insight into a few of the more controversial questions science teachers face when the relationship between science and faith arises in the classroom.

"THE CONFLICT THESIS"

In the background of much of the confusion regarding faith and science is the so-called Conflict Thesis. It is not only religions that tell creation myths. Every culture, including our own, has stories it tells about how the world works and how it got to be the way that it is. We have seen some aspects of this in our chapter on history (chapter 6). A key element of modernity's creation mythology is the story of science overcoming religious superstition. This myth is so common that even many religious people take it for granted. The problem is that almost none of it is true.

The basic outline of this myth is familiar. Once upon a time, medieval Europeans — and, presumably, everyone else who did not have modern science — lived in darkness and ignorance. Then, some brave souls, led by the likes of Galileo Galilei, developed the scientific method and threw off the chains of superstition, leading to our modern rational and scientific worldview in which reason has replaced faith and science has replaced religion.

We can distinguish two different kinds of claims at the heart of this myth, one methodological and one historical. The methodological claim is that science is the best (and perhaps the only) way to know what is true about the world and that religious ways of knowing are tantamount to superstition. In this view, faith is at least naïve, and maybe positively irresponsible. The corresponding historical claim is that scientific knowledge is slowly but surely replacing religious knowledge in one domain after another and relegating religion to the dustbin of history or, at the very least, to the sphere of private belief where it can do little harm. Remarkably, in order to substantiate this claim, various historical episodes have had to be invented.

One such yarn is that Columbus's contemporaries believed in a flat earth and worried he would fall off the edge of the planet if he sailed west. Not only did medieval and early modern Europeans know the earth was round (just read Dante's *Inferno*, where hell is placed at the center of a spherical earth), but they had a fairly good sense of its circumference. It was actually Columbus whose calculations on this point were mistaken. He only dared begin his voyage west because he believed Asia to be much closer by sea than it actually was. And he was fortunate to strike land somewhere between Portugal and Japan, or he would have run out of supplies. The flat-earth mythology associated with this episode came into vogue hundreds of years after the fact, popularized in anti-Catholic propaganda.

Another fabrication is that the great library at Alexandria was destroyed by fanatical, anti-science Christian mobs, setting the progress of science back by hundreds of years. This too is utterly false — and perpetuated in popular culture with expressly anti-Christian intentions. It is not even entirely clear when the library was destroyed. Part of it was burnt by Roman troops forty years before Jesus was born. In later times, it went into decline, and the best guess we have is that it was a casualty of one or another subsequent Roman attacks on the city. There was a series of ugly riots involving Christians and others in the city at one point, but it had nothing to do with science or the great library.

GALILEO

One episode in the science versus religion narrative that has some basis in history is the so-called Galileo Affair. But even that story is told with significant embellishment in order to make it do the work the myth requires of it. Galileo's instincts were right (the earth did go around the sun), but his science was wrong. He could not demonstrate the truth of his hypothesis. And the best scientists of his time knew it. More than that, the head of the Inquisition, St. Robert Bellarmine, granted that, if Galileo's hypotheses were to be scientifically proven, certain passages of Scripture that seemed to put the earth at the center of the universe would need to be reinterpreted. That is to say, the Church was not all that troubled by Galileo's hypothesis. It just wasn't going to endorse as-yet-unproven conclusions.

In any case, if the Galileo Affair is supposed to be emblematic of a larger conflict between science and Christianity, it should be one of many examples. The fact that it stands virtually alone is itself instructive. The Galileo Affair was not an example of the typical relationship between science and religion, but an idiosyncratic event that had more to do with personalities and politics than with any inherent conflict between science and religion. Moreover, Galileo himself never dreamt that his scientific hypotheses undermined religion. In fact, he basically agreed with Bellarmine about the religious implications of the notion that the earth goes around the sun rather than vice versa. Which is to say, he didn't think those implications changed much about the claims of Christianity at all — something that promoters of this mythology prefer not to mention.

In this Galileo was far from alone. None of the leading lights of the scientific revolution imagined themselves to be working against the Christian worldview of early modern Europe. That neither Copernicus nor Galileo nor Kepler found their science to be in conflict with their faith is telling. It is hard to make the case that faith and science are intrinsically opposed when the heroes of your narrative all reject that conclusion by their lives. Moreover, the scientific breakthroughs of folks like Copernicus and Galileo did not run directly counter to the worldview they inherited, as we are usually told, but rather built upon it. Copernicus's astronomical system, in which the earth went around the sun (heliocentrism) rather than vice versa (geocentrism), was only theoretically possible after a whole series of scientific developments in late medieval Europe. The common presentation of Copernicus's work as a "revolution," completely overturning the ideas of his predecessors, is part of the myth of progress. In Catholic schools, at least, a more nuanced story should be told.

THE PATH TO COPERNICUS

It will be instructive to take a brief look at this history.* The development of science stalled out in ancient Greece largely because various proposals that seemed logical (e.g., that heavier objects fall faster than lighter ones or that vacuums are impossible) were accepted without ever being tested. These notions held sway for centuries. But they started to be questioned by medieval theologians. And in 1277 the archbishop of Paris condemned a series of propositions from Aristotle, including the idea that vacuums were impossible. From a modern point of view, a churchman condemning scientific propositions looks positively backwards. But these *weren't* exactly scientific propositions. They were, rather, philosophical conclusions that were actually impeding science. And the upshot of their condemnation was a flourishing of scientific inquiry. If anything leading to modern science can be called a "revolution," it might well be this list of condemnations.

If certain long-held, but unproven, conclusions need not be held any longer, science could get to work. And the theoretical possibility that space was, in fact, a vacuum, led to a whole series of hypotheses — that the planets do not need some external power source pushing them through the ether, that the earth spins on its axis, that heliocentrism is at least theoretically possible — that made Copernicus's advance possible. Moreover, as every student of the history of science knows, Copernicus's system was itself rather incomplete, and further refinements, particularly Kepler's discovery of the elliptical orbits of the planets, were necessary to really make it work.

There is no question that the shift from geocentrism to he-

---

* Every Catholic science teacher (I am tempted to just say "every Catholic"!) should read Stephen Barr's brief booklet, *Science and Religion: The Myth of Conflict*. It narrates this episode exceptionally well and is the best short introduction to the basic questions of science from a Catholic perspective I have seen.

liocentrism was important. But it was not so radical a change as the story we usually hear suggests. It was one step of many made by several scientists over several centuries — one which depended on and led to other steps. What is more, the system that was being overturned in this process was not a system based on the Bible or Church teaching, but on ancient Greek thought. Our students have almost certainly been given the impression that the shift to heliocentrism is a classic example of science replacing religion as a way of knowing about the world. They need to learn how to see through such nonsense.

Medieval Europe had used the Ptolemaic system for centuries not because it was biblical (in the Old Testament the earth is not a sphere, but a land mass on pillars covered by a dome!), but because it was the best science available at the time. Indeed, it could even be argued that the picture of the earth we see in the Book of Genesis was also based on the best science available at the time *it* was written. And so, the shift from a flat earth on pillars under a dome to the Ptolemaic system to the Copernican system is not a story of science refuting religion, but of Judeo-Christian religion consistently accepting and integrating the best available science from the ambient culture.

Contrary to the Conflict Thesis, religion is largely untroubled by scientific developments because religion and science are complementary rather than conflicting ways of knowing. If religion really was only an attempt to explain naturalistic phenomena without recourse to the scientific method, as our modern mythology imagines, then the discoveries of the sciences *would* slowly crowd out any need for God or religion. But religion is concerned with very different kinds of questions than science is. As Rabbi Jonathan Sacks puts it, "Science takes things apart to tell us how they work; religion brings things together to show us what they mean." Religious texts like the first few chapters of Genesis are interested in questions of human meaning. Only if we misread such texts as primarily concerned with natural phenomena do science and religion appear to come into conflict.

BEWARE THE "GOD OF THE GAPS"

In the mythology of modernity, religion was never more than an attempt to provide explanations for naturalistic phenomena. Before we could understand the natural mechanisms behind things such as earthquakes or drought, the story goes, humans simply attributed such things to the will of the gods. As we come to learn about plate tectonics and water cycles, such supernatural explanations become superfluous. As this process advances, to the point where physicists can hypothesize about the beginnings of our physical universe with no reference to divine powers, it begins to look, to paraphrase the eminent physicist Stephen Hawking, like there is nothing left for God to do.

Christians can unwittingly contribute to this kind of misunderstanding. When, for example, we point to the current lack of scientific understanding or consensus around a given issue as evidence for God, we are digging our own graves. If abiogenesis — the emergence of life from nonlife — is not currently well understood, for instance, and Christians seize upon this fact and claim that the emergence of life from nonlife is evidence that God reached into creation and miraculously tweaked matter to create life, what happens to God when the process becomes better understood? Such a "God of the Gaps" gets smaller and smaller as our scientific understanding grows. And it is we who have put God and science in a zero-sum game.

But this God of the Gaps has very little in common with the God of the Bible and of Christian tradition. Traditional arguments for God's existence have never relied on using God as a substitute for scientific explanations. This is why a movement like Intelligent Design — which posits that there are various steps in the course of evolution where God needed to step in — does more harm than good. Not only does it bet God's existence on science being unable to answer properly scientific questions (a bet whose odds can only get worse with time), it completely misunderstands the traditional Christian view of God's relationship with creation and reduces God to one more cause within creation instead of the reason anything even exists at all. As pious and faithful as it might seem to do so, we do not do our students any favors if we substitute God for properly scientific causality in science class.

Far from being an obstacle modern science had to overcome, Christianity was an essential prerequisite to its development. If science and Christianity were, as the Conflict Thesis would have us believe, mortal enemies, it is very odd indeed that the one place in human history that science emerges is in intensely Christian early modern Europe. Not only were the vast majority of early modern scientists faithful Christians, but their scientific endeavors built upon foundations laid by Christian theologians in the centuries before what has come to be called, a little misleadingly, "the scientific revolution." Indeed, many of these theologians were also natural philosophers — that is to say, in the parlance of the day, scientists.

In the universities of medieval Europe, the study of philosophy, including natural philosophy (i.e., science), preceded the study of theology. Consequently, theologians were the most scientifically literate group in society. St. Thomas Aquinas's teacher, St .Albert the Great, was not only a great theologian, but one of the leading scientists of his day. Roger Bacon, often credited with developing the scientific method, was a friar and a student of the great scientist-bishop of Lincoln, Robert Grosseteste. And these examples are not the exception, but the rule. That Copernicus was a canon at a cathedral was not at all out of the ordinary. Among his scientific forerunners were monks, priests, and bishops. One of the great scientific minds of this era was Nicholas of Cusa, a cardinal, who even speculated about the possibility of a multiverse!

All of which raises an important question. Science does not simply appear out of nowhere. For it to emerge as a systematic way of exploring the world, a whole series of philosophical prerequisites are necessary. And these prerequisites have only ever come together in one time and place in human history. What was it about the worldview of Christian Europe that made the development of science possible?

PREREQUISITES FOR SCIENCE IN MEDIEVAL THEOLOGY

As for theology ... it is a sophisticated, highly rational discipline that has its roots in Judaism and in Greek philosophy and has been fully developed only in Christianity. The pursuit of knowledge was inherent in theology as efforts to more fully understand God were extended to include God's creation — thus inaugurating an academic enterprise known as natural philosophy, defined as the study of nature and of natural phenomena.

RODNEY STARK

The first thing to note is the Judeo-Christian belief that God is radically other than creation. As we saw at the beginning of Part II, the biblical insistence on God's transcendence demystifies the created order — often seen as at least semi-divine in many worldviews — and makes it susceptible to scientific investigation. Relatedly, the Bible insists that creation is not chaotic and arbitrary, but intelligibly ordered, reflecting the mind of the Creator. "The heavens," the psalmist sings, "are telling the glory of God" (Ps 19:1). Science is not possible unless the object of study is predictable and coherent. If an experiment might get a different result every day, it does not tell us much.

And Christianity not only teaches that God and creation are rational and orderly, but also that humans are uniquely equipped to engage with such order. In exploring the biblical teaching that humans are made in the image and likeness of God, Christian theology has placed a particular emphasis on human rationality. Though contemporary theology has helpfully supplemented this with a complementary emphasis on relationality, for much of Christian history — and certainly for that period leading up to the scientific revolution — the most emphasized aspect of being made in God's image was being rational.

This emphasis on rationality was, in fact, at the heart of the whole enterprise of Christian theology even before it became the heart of science. Indeed, the case can be made that theology itself was a necessary prerequisite for science. For starters, Christian theology teaches specific content that makes science possible: that God is the transcendent Creator and that creation is not divine; that creation is orderly and intelligible; that humans are made rational in God's image. Moreover, the practice of Christian theology is itself formally analogous to science in important ways. The classic definition of theology, from St. Anselm of Canterbury, is "faith seeking understanding." This runs counter to what many today imagine faith means — namely, believing *without* understanding. But Christians have always insisted that faith should make sense. This does not mean we think we can fit the infinite God into the finite box of our minds. But it does mean that whatever we can understand of the infinite God will not be absurd, incoherent, or meaningless. Christians believe that we can know and say true things about God.

Christian theology, then, emerges as the highly rational enterprise of exploring what we can and cannot say about God given what we know from divine revelation. And it is here that the parallels with science become instructive. Both theology and science start with data that is *given*, explore that data with fitting conceptual and analytical tools, and then make further hypotheses to advance knowledge that can and must be tested against the initially given reality. Theologians may make new proposals, for instance, but those proposals will be checked for their consistency with Scripture and Tradition and even, if it becomes necessary, subjected to the judgment of the magisterium of the Church. The theologian, then, is responsible to Revelation in a way analogous to the way the scientist is responsible to the experimental data.

It is important to recognize, of course, that the *kind of data* given at the beginning of each process is not exactly the same. Theology begins with Revelation, though not uncritically so. An important branch of theology is fundamental theology, which explores whether and how it is reasonable to recognize and accept any proposed Divine Revelation. Science begins with experimental data, derived from observing the material world. But, again, not uncritically so. Without a sophisticated and self-critical philosophy of science, it is very easy for observations to lead to unwarranted conclusions and for experiments to be poorly designed. Both theology and science need to be aware of their own presuppositions and methodology in order to function well.

Such parallels go a long way to explaining why so many progenitors of the scientific revolution were theologians. Not only were theologians the most scientifically literate group in medieval Europe, but theology at this time was highly philosophical and self-reflective, becoming ever more conscious of methodological questions and thinking about how knowledge — any knowledge — is justified. That a group so intensely interested in method in theology should reflect on their practice of natural philosophy in a way that led to the scientific method is hardly surprising.

Theologians had distinguished, for instance, between theology proper, whose starting point was Revelation, and what is sometimes called "natural theology." It is not "theology proper" because it tries to understand what we can know about God from looking at creation itself, before we accept any claims of Divine Revelation. Theologians taught that, before God gave us the Bible, he gave us the Book of Nature. And in that book too, God was revealed. If we were to look at Thomas Aquinas's famous five arguments for God's existence, for instance, we would notice that none of them depend on any belief in Divine Revelation. That would be putting the cart before the horse. Rather, what we can know about God by using our reason to reflect on creation is preliminary to the question of whether any such God might reveal himself to us. This is not yet science, of course, but a worldview that is making these distinctions is just the kind of worldview that science needs to get any traction.

PRIMARY AND SECONDARY CAUSALITY

An even more specific prerequisite for the emergence of scientific thinking is the distinction medieval theologians made between primary and secondary causality. It is a common mistake to imagine God as one element in a larger system, as one being among many, however powerful. One form that mistake can take is to imagine God as one *cause* among many. It is this kind of thinking that leads to the question, "If God created everything, then who created God?" Now, this is a perceptive question from a bright elementary school student. And exploring it honestly can truly deepen understanding. Coming from ostensibly serious public intellectuals, however, it is rarely more than a disingenuous "gotcha" question.

The third of Aquinas's arguments for God's existence highlights that nothing we encounter with our senses can account for itself — that such things are "contingent." They must, therefore, have their source outside themselves. This argument does not simply posit one more such contingent thing as the explanation for all the other contingent things. Rather, the argument is that a reality made only of contingent things, even an infinite series of contingent things, is incoherent. There must be not merely some earlier, more powerful thing, but another kind of "thing" altogether. *If there is contingent being, there must be some necessary being.* Notice how this philosophical argument lines up with the radical biblical distinction between creation and Creator.

Theologians recognized that a God who is not one more being among other beings was also not just one more cause among other causes. And just as God's being transcends created being, God's causality transcends the causality proper to creation. God's creation of the universe, then, is not in competition with any scientific explanation of the beginning of the universe. These are, instead, answers to two different kinds of questions. In a Catholic science class, this distinction, first insisted upon by medieval theologians, must be consistently upheld. God, whose nature it is *to be*, gives being to creation, not merely at its beginning, but always and everywhere. Thomas Aquinas even argued that, were we to grant that the universe was eternal, it would still need a creator because even an infinite series of contingent realities cannot account for its own existence. God is the answer to the question "Why is there something rather than nothing?" Science, on the other hand, is interested in predicting the behavior of various observable somethings, even if those somethings are merely quantum fluctuations in a vacuum. To imagine that scientific explanations about quantum particles popping into existence make God superfluous is a category mistake.

Theologians call this giving of being, which is proper only to God, primary causality. They distinguish this radically from the kind of causality — secondary causality — that is in effect between the different elements of creation. And these two kinds of causality are so different from one another that they cannot be in competition with one another. What this means for the development of science is that *secondary causes are treated as causes in their own right that operate without any divine interference.* Such a bracketing of God or any other supernatural explanation — which atheists rightly identify as essential to the scientific method — was first proposed by Christian theologians! Without this distinction, science cannot get off the ground.

As technical as all this may seem, we are actually quite familiar with the basic distinction at play. We tell our kids, for example, both that babies come from a loving act of a mother and a father and that babies are a gift from God. That the second is true does nothing to deny the scientific reality of the first. No one argues that, because we know how sperm and eggs work, God does not exist. God is not in competition with parents in the procreation of children, but is upholding created being — and with it created causality — so that it can be itself. God gives us children *through* the loving act of parents without interfering in that act at all.

Perhaps we can see this more clearly if we consider that even within the realm of secondary causality there are different levels that can transcend one another without being in competition. One day my daughter Dorothy, when she was about seven years old, asked me how it is that Mommy and Daddy make a baby if God makes babies. Dorothy loves coloring, so I asked whether her pictures are colored by the markers or by Dorothy. She immediately saw that she and the markers were not in competition, but that both, each in their own way, truly colored the pictures.

We can also see this in the variety of possible correct answers to the question "Why?" Let's say that we see a car driving down the street come to a sudden halt. We may well ask why that happened. One perfectly true answer is that the car stopped because, when the driver stepped on the brake pedal, pressurized fluid moved through the brake lines, causing the brake pads to be applied to the rotors, and the resulting friction took all the energy from the car's forward momentum. Another perfectly true answer is that the driver saw a child chase a ball across the road. There is no need to choose between these answers, or even to find some middle ground between them. Instead, we can simply affirm both of them as true without qualification. This is because the second cause transcends the first.

EVOLUTION

If, in reading the last section, your mind started turning to the question of evolution, congratulations! Because it is precisely this kind of thinking about causality that made the theory of evolution a relatively minor problem for the Catholic Church when it emerged. Yes, there are Christians who imagine that evolution is somehow contrary to the teaching of Scripture. But when they do this, they are reading Scripture quite differently than the Catholic Church has always read it. And yes, the Catholic Church did have some serious questions about evolution. But those related not so much to the scientific theory itself, but rather to the kinds of philosophical conclusions that some folks imagined followed from it.

Contrary to the common presumption that the Church has always read the Bible in a fundamentalist manner and was only recently forced into more poetic or literary readings by the advancement of the sciences, the Church has always recognized that Scripture is made up of many genres that each deserve to be read according to their own rules. This is, by the way, what the Church means by reading Scripture "literally," namely, to read it according to the conventions of a given literary genre so as to properly understand the intentions of the author. In Church teaching, this is contrasted with reading "literalistically," which is taking everything at face value even when the context and genre manifestly exclude such a reading. Even children know that stories with talking animals are not meant to be read in a literalistic manner. The snake in the garden is a dead giveaway that what we are reading is not intended as a strict historical account nor as a science textbook.

Sixteen-hundred years ago, in *On the Literal Meaning of Genesis*, Saint Augustine wrote:

> Usually, even a non-Christian knows something about the earth, the heavens, and the other elements of the world, about the motion and orbit of the stars and even their size and relative positions, about the predictable eclipses of the sun and moon, the cycles of the years and the seasons, about the kinds of animals, shrubs, stones, and so forth, and this knowledge he holds to as being certain from reason and experience. Now, it is a disgraceful and dangerous thing for an infidel to hear a Christian, presumably giving the meaning of Holy Scripture, talking nonsense on these topics; and we should take all means to prevent such an embarrassing situation, in which people show up vast ignorance in a Christian and laugh it to scorn.

From the beginning, the great theologians of the Christian tradition have advocated reading Scripture in a way that comports with the best science of the day! Literary readings of Scripture are not a retreat of religion in the face of science, as the Conflict Thesis would have it, but the way the Church has always read the Bible.

What is perhaps even more surprising is that the biblical view of God's relationship with creation, codified by medieval theologians in their distinction between primary and secondary causality, led both Saint Augustine and St. Thomas Aquinas to say things that sound remarkably like evolution long before Darwin came on the scene. From today's vantage point it is quite stunning to read Augustine teaching that: "It is therefore, *causally* that Scripture has said that *earth brought forth* the crops and trees, in the sense that *it received the power* of bringing them forth. In the earth from the beginning, in what I might call the roots of time, God created *what was to be in times to come*" (emphasis added). Several hundred years later, Thomas Aquinas could write: "Nature is nothing but the plan of some art, namely a divine one, put into things themselves, by which those things move towards a concrete end: as if the man who builds up a ship could give to the pieces of wood that they could move by themselves to produce the form of the ship."

If this is the traditional Catholic attitude towards the relationship between God and creation, it is no wonder that St. John Henry Newman, the most important theologian living when Darwin published *On the Origin of Species*, could write with equanimity: "Mr. Darwin's theory need not then to be atheistical, be it true or not; it may simply be suggesting a larger idea of Divine Prescience and Skill." Notice, in particular, that Newman is completely untroubled by the suggestion that the earth is much older than previously assumed. That this is somehow a problem for the Bible does not even seem to occur to him.

Science teachers, these quotes deserve a spot on the walls of your classrooms! Students need to know that acknowledging the truth of evolution is not the Church retreating before modernity, but something in serene harmony with the Church's long-stand-ing theological tradition.

It is, in point of fact, harder to find a better example to il-lustrate primary and secondary causality than God's creating *ex nihilo*, on the one hand, and the theory of evolution, on the other. Which is precisely why the Dominican theologians behind the YouTube course *Aquinas 101* used it in their video on primary and secondary causality. Something at least *like* evolution is almost how you would expect the creation of the biblical God to operate. It is no wonder, then, that the Catholic Church, including all the recent popes and the virtually unanimous chorus of the theologi-cal guild, is able to accept evolution as a scientific theory without qualm. There are, nevertheless, a few cautions to be observed.

EVOLUTION*ISM*

While evolution as a scientific theory poses no threat to Catholic faith, we need to be attentive to what some people claim the theo-ry of evolution *means*. Remember, science deals with questions of how things work, not what they mean. If someone tells you what a given scientific theory means, they are no longer doing science. To distinguish the scientific theory of evolution from these kinds of unwarranted philosophical conclusions, many refer to the larger collection of nonscientific beliefs that are often attached to evo-lution as "evolutionism." It is not evolution itself, but evolution*ism*, that insists, for example, that science has proved the Bible is false, or has ruled out the need for a Creator. Ironically, the world's most famous atheists and the religious fundamentalists they love to rid-icule are at one on this point. Both groups read the creation nar-ratives in the Bible as if they were intended as science lessons and then conclude that evolution and Christianity are incompatible.

Catholic science teachers, accordingly, need to be aware of certain dangers as we teach evolution. First of all, we should take great care that when we tell students that Catholics don't take the Bible *literally* (though it's better to say we don't take it "literalistically" and explain the difference), they don't conclude that this means that we don't take the Bible *seriously*. I was once teaching a group of new teachers a course on sacraments. When we turned to the Gospels to read certain key passages related to Baptism or the Eucharist, they were confused when I used those passages to draw theological conclusions about the sacraments because they had just been taught in their Scripture class that Catholics don't take the Bible literally! The attempt to teach them a more nuanced, Catholic approach to Scripture had inadvertently convinced them that the Bible was not a reliable source at all.

But reading the first chapters of Genesis as a science textbook is actually taking the Bible *less seriously* than reading it as it was meant to be read. It is the fundamentalist reading that waters down Scripture, ignoring its deep human and religious significance and making it about geology or biology. The single best cure I know for this error is reading Joseph Ratzinger's *'In the Beginning …': A Catholic Understanding of the Story of Creation and the Fall*. It is impossible to read Ratzinger's reflections on the creation narratives and come away with the idea that a literalistic reading is the more serious option.

Second, we need to be clear that when we say the Church has no problem with evolution, we do not mean that the Church has no problem with the kinds of assertions people often make using evolution. Not only does evolution not disprove God or the Bible, it also does not mean that each of us is nothing but a kind of cosmic accident. In his first homily as pope, Benedict XVI proclaimed: "We are not some casual and meaningless product of evolution. Each of us is the result of a thought of God. Each of us is willed, each of us is loved, each of us is necessary."

It is clear from the rest of his work and ministry that the pope was not rejecting evolution as a scientific theory. Like John

Paul II before him and Francis after, in all his writing on the topic, Benedict consistently holds that evolution is the best scientific explanation we have for the shape of life on earth and that, as a scientific theory, it poses no threat to faith. Rather, he is rejecting the conclusion that many draw from evolution, namely that, because the mechanism of evolution includes randomness, we are nothing more than the products of mere chance, and that any meaning or purpose we might seek for our lives is illusory. Our students may well have been given the impression that evolution means we are nothing more than cosmic accidents. When our Faith tells them that they are each willed and loved by God, some will find consolation, though perhaps by rejecting evolution. Others may conclude that religion is just wishful thinking for those who cannot face the hard truth of the matter.

CHANCE AND PURPOSE

O you mysterious galaxies. ... I see you, I calculate you, I understand you, I study you and I discover you, I penetrate you and I gather you. From you I take light and make it knowledge, I take movement and make it wisdom, I take sparkling colors and make them poetry; I take you stars in my hands and, trembling in the oneness of my being, I raise you above yourselves and offer you in prayer to the Creator, that through me alone you stars can worship.

SERVANT OF GOD ENRICO MEDI,
CATHOLIC ASTROPHYSICIST

So, what should we teach our students? Is it possible that we are each loved and willed by God if there is genuine randomness built into the universe? Can God effectively will each of us if our existence is dependent on so many radically contingent factors? Let's begin by noticing that this is not a new problem introduced by the theory of evolution. Christian theology was already keenly aware of the role of chance in creation. In his *Summa Contra Gentiles* (Book III, Chapter 74), for example, Thomas Aquinas argues "that divine providence does not exclude fortune and chance." In fact, in the course of this chapter, Aquinas demonstrates that providence actually *requires* chance because "it would be contrary to the essential character of divine providence if all things occurred by necessity."

We don't need to know about evolution to know that if your mother and father had never met — or even if they had met, married, gone out for a nice dinner, had a glass of wine, started cuddling and whispering sweet nothings, and then gotten interrupted by a late-night knock on the door — you would have never been born. Moreover, long before the theory of evolution, theology had been thinking about the relationship between God's providence and human freedom. How, in short, can God's will be assured if humans are truly free? The problem is analogous. How can God's will be done if there is genuine chance in creation?

Here again we see the relevance of different levels of causality that can transcend one another. Thomas Aquinas teaches that God does not achieve his will *in spite of* human freedom, but precisely *through* human freedom. As we have already seen, good parents and teachers are more than capable of working through the freedom of children or students. In fact, once you get good at it, you realize it is much easier than working against their freedom. Theologians note that a God who can achieve his own ends through human freedom is actually more impressive than a God who is reduced to simply overpowering us.

How might this insight apply to randomness in creation? Experience teaches us that it is possible to achieve predictable, desired results not simply in spite of randomness, but even through it. Do casinos need to load the dice in order to make money at the craps table? Of course not. The simple fact that they are dice means that certain statistical patterns will emerge over time. The more tosses of the dice, the closer every number will come to having turned up one-sixth of the time. Put this in combination with some more dice and some well-considered rules for the game, and you can use genuine randomness to guarantee that, despite some losses along the way, the house always wins in the end.

When we design games with elements of chance, that chance does not impede the goals of those games. Rather, the goals of the games are achieved *through* chance. If we humans can transcend randomness in order to achieve our ends, surely it is not too much for God! Take the phenomenon known as "convergent evolution." Given the parameters of creation, i.e., the rules of the game, life will find similar solutions to similar problems. Bats did not evolve from birds, nor birds from bats. Rather, flight evolved in both birds and bats because of the nature of the problem that the ancestors of both bats and birds were trying to solve and the range of options available to them in the world as it exists. Or take the evolution of eyes. Eyes take many forms in the animal world. Evolutionary biologists tell us that they have evolved independently many times over. Why? Because light behaves the way that it does! And so, different organisms' optimal responses to light will resemble one another. (For more on this, see Catholic biologist Daniel Kuebler's excellent video, *The Purposeful Universe*, from the Magis Center.)

Did God need to rig the game of evolution in order for humans to emerge? Not in the sense of interfering along the way because the randomness in the system kept leading to inconvenient results. No, God is more like the game designer who can set the initial parameters such that, no matter what happens with the dice on this or that roll, certain outcomes will predictably emerge. But, notice, even this analogy falls short. If we can transcend randomness with purpose, so can God, but to an infinitely greater degree. The analogy serves to show that randomness does not render God's will ineffective. It does not — because no analogy can — plumb the true depths of God's transcendence or his providential love. You and I could not will an individual human person from all eternity despite genuine randomness. God can.

But there is more. Not only is genuine chance in creation not a problem for God's providence, it actually supports the Christian worldview. Since ancient times, materialistic determinism (the opposite of chance!) has been a challenge to Christianity. The argument, in its simplest form, is that matter is going to do what matter is going to do, and so all outcomes in the universe were already fixed by its initial conditions. In this picture, human freedom is only an illusion. If, on the other hand, there is genuine chance in material reality, there is also openness to different potential outcomes. The freedom humans experience in the realm of spirit finds in chance an analogy in the realm of matter. The Christian conviction that our choices are real and that they matter fits much more comfortably in a world that is open-ended than in one that is strictly determined. Chance is not a threat to a Christian worldview, but an ally.

A final note on teaching evolution. The Church has been clear that, when it comes to the evolution of human persons, the theory cannot account for everything that makes us human. Humans are unique creatures, made up of a body and a rational soul. While evolution is the best explanation we have for the emergence of our bodies as they exist, evolution applies only to matter. Not being material, the human soul is not the kind of thing that can evolve. Rather, the Church insists, God creates each human soul individually at the moment we begin to exist as independent beings. And so, whatever form our bodies take — and whether we trace that to the genes we get from our parents or to the basic body plan we share with all vertebrates or all the way back to the DNA we share with all life on this planet — it remains the case that God wills each of us for our own sake and grants us not simply being in general, but the specific being that we, as beloved sons and daughters made in his image, are.

SCIENTISM

Science can purify religion from error and superstition; religion can purify science from idolatry and false absolutes. Each can draw the other into a wider world, a world in which both can flourish.

POPE ST. JOHN PAUL II

Because science is so good at what it does, it is very tempting to absolutize it. If science can tell us with such incredible depth and precision about things like DNA or quantum mechanics, should we not also rely on it to assess other matters, like the beauty of a poem, or the justice of a verdict? Some people think so. They imagine that matters like beauty and justice are as susceptible to the scientific method as the physical structures of our universe. Such a view typically follows from a materialism that imagines that things like beauty or justice are, in the final analysis, only epiphenomena of material reality. Other people who absolutize science have a different take. They conclude that, since things like the beauty of a poem or the justice of a verdict are *not* susceptible to the scientific method, such things are not true in any meaningful sense. They are, at best, useful fictions.

Imagining that science is the only way to any true knowledge is called scientism. And it is a form of fundamentalism. It arbitrarily narrows reality down to what science can study and then imagines that science somehow disproves the existence of other elements of reality. What Catholics (and many others) would understand as spiritual realities, things like justice or beauty or even the principle of identity that makes a thing to be what it is despite changes to its physical structure, are either explained away as extrapolations of the merely material, and hence ultimately reducible to the material, or as attempts to make meaning where there is no meaning.

Such dismissals are not compelling. In addition to telling us that the things that intuitively seem to matter most in life really don't matter much at all, thereby presenting radically unsatisfying answers to the basic questions of human existence, the whole exercise is circular and self-refuting. Science rightly narrows its scope to deal strictly with material reality, with no outside interference allowed. Such focus is highly effective, and science could hardly function without it. But to then suppose that the narrow object of this focus is the sum total of reality is to mistake one's (wholly justified) methodological presupposition for a (quite unjustified) conclusion. That science rightly focuses on the material to the exclusion of all else does not mean there is nothing else. What is more, scientism is itself immaterial and cannot be proven by science. Even those who advocate for it are implicitly acknowledging a reality beyond what science can study.

SALVATION BY TECHNOLOGY?

It is not science that redeems man: man is redeemed by love.

POPE BENEDICT XVI

Every worldview has an eschatology — that is to say, a story of where the world is headed. While scientism may imagine that the end of each human person is simply to have their molecules recycled in the ecosystem, it can also tell a larger story about the human future. One such story is salvation by technology. Human technology is truly incredible. Humans have put astronauts on the moon and may well put them on Mars in our lifetime. An average Joe takes for granted flying across the globe, talking to people anywhere in the world in real time, receiving routine medical treatment for diseases that have killed millions of his forebears, and plugging his phone into outlets powered by splitting atoms!

From a Catholic point of view, technology is part of the human stewardship of creation. God built incredible potential into reality, and humans have managed to develop that potential in remarkable ways. Indeed, the development of that potential is a way — not unlike art — that we image God's stunning creativity. Moreover, while technology can give us a sense of incredible power, of overcoming boundaries, closer reflection teaches us that technology is much more a case of working with creation than working against it. We cannot do simply anything. We can only do what is possible in creation as it is. And when we ignore the deeper realities of creation (whether physical or spiritual), our technologies can lead to devastation.

As impressive as technology is and as many problems as it has solved and will solve in the future, technology is not able to save us. Our deepest problems are not technical, but spiritual. No matter how many diseases we cure, no matter what sources of clean energy we tap, we will not address the human need for meaning, for love, for forgiveness and redemption. Indeed, as long as our spiritual problems go unaddressed, even the most amazing technology will be deeply ambiguous.

Social media, for example, can achieve real goods, but many today wonder if we might be better off without it. While it can connect us and give us access to information and entertainment, it seems to have amplified many of our worst tendencies, spreading lies and even violence, dividing families and communities, and contributing to an epidemic of anxiety and depression, particularly among the young. Having healthy and productive relationships online requires real spiritual discipline. Most of us have had to learn new skills and work hard to develop some quite specific virtues to navigate this new environment. It is easy to imagine, when a new technology emerges, all the good it can accomplish. But we cannot ignore the human factor. As amazing as it is to generate clean energy by splitting atoms, a mushroom cloud hovers in the background.

A Catholic education needs to offer a wholistic picture of the world, one in which science and technology take their rightful place, but in which they are neither absolutized nor idealized. As Pope St. John Paul II wrote: "Religion can purify science from idolatry and false absolutes." A Catholic education that thus purifies science, and produces scientists, doctors, engineers, and others who can appreciate the role of science in human flourishing while also seeing the broader picture will be of great service to humanity.

Assignment Idea: Exploring Catholic Scientists

To counter the notion that science and religion are inherently in conflict, very little is as compelling as learning about the life, work, and ideas of high-level practitioners of science who are also believers. Have students do a report on a Catholic scientist. The reports should include an investigation of the scientist's historical and scientific context. For example, Galileo's context is very different from that of Brother Guy Consulmagno S.J., astrophysicist and current director of the Vatican's observatory, not only in terms of the stage of development of the sciences themselves, but also in the attitudes about science and religion common among their contemporaries. Reports should include a careful exploration of the scientist's specific contributions to their field and the significance of those contributions. Finally, they should include a study of the particular scientist's thinking on the relationship between science and faith. These reports could be written or presented or both. This could be an especially effective cross-curricular assignment with history and/or religion.

KEY TAKEAWAYS

The question of the relationship between science and faith is one of the most pressing issues in the Church's relationship with young people. Science teachers in Catholic schools have an essential role to play here.

Much confusion is caused by the so-called Conflict Hypothesis that invokes several bogus or misinterpreted historical events in its attempt to demonstrate the incompatibility of science and religion. Catholic science teachers need to know how to engage with it.

Far from being an impediment to be overcome, Christian theology actually provided the intellectual and cultural prerequisites necessary for the development of modern science.

One reason the Catholic Church has had so little trouble with the theory of evolution is the distinctions made by medieval theologians, like the one between primary and secondary causality, that led to the development of modern science in the first place.

The Catholic Church has no trouble with evolution as a scientific theory but wants to be careful about certain nonscientific conclusions people often draw from it.

Genuine chance in the natural order is not contrary to God's providence and does not make creation, let alone individual human beings, into cosmic accidents.

The incredible power and promise of science must not blind us to the value of other ways of encountering the truth.

Chapter 9
Civics and Social Studies

In Matthew 22:21, when Jesus is asked about the legitimacy of Jews paying taxes to their Roman occupiers, he famously answers, "Give therefore to the emperor the things that are the emperor's, and to God the things that are God's." This answer has two important layers, though we often catch only the first. On the surface, this is a straightforward exhortation for Christians to live as good citizens in whichever society they find themselves, to recognize legitimate political authority, and to contribute to the common good. This is true enough, insofar as it goes. But, in a Catholic school, we will be doing our students and our society a great disservice if we do not attend to the second layer. The emperor was worshipped in ancient Rome. Indeed, persecution of the early Christians often hinged on their refusal of such worship. Which brings us to the deeper and more subversive meaning of what Jesus is saying: *Caesar is not God!*

The explicit goal of civics and social studies classes is to prepare students for responsible citizenship and healthy participation in their society. It is to prepare them to give to Caesar what is Caesar's. The difficulty, from a Catholic point of view, is that, sometimes implicitly, sometimes explicitly, it is all too easy to treat membership in the nation, and its political and economic system, as our highest loyalty. Civics class may not explicitly ask us to worship an emperor, but it can very easily lead us to imagine that our identity as Americans or Canadians takes priority over our identity as Christians. Even if this is not said directly, it can be implied in a thousand small ways.

Have we ever, for example, been unwittingly convinced that our citizenship in the nation state is a public matter, but our religious convictions are merely private? Have we believed that it is somehow inappropriate in our democracy to "impose" our religious views on our fellow citizens? If so, we are probably giving to Caesar, not just what is Caesar's, but what is God's as well.

A civics or social studies class in a Catholic school is the ideal place to push back against these false notions, and we will consider the question of the role of faith in public life in more detail below. But there are other, perhaps more subtle, instances where what is taught in these classes can run counter to a fully Catholic worldview. For instance, every nation has a vested interest in convincing its citizens that its form of government is the most legitimate form. And one of the most important places for a state to communicate this notion is in schools. Similarly, it is in the interest of those who benefit from the current economic paradigm to extol its virtues to the broader population, and they are happy to influence curricula in that direction. To this end, alternatives to the status quo, whether political or economic, are often presented as "straw men." All of which serves to stunt our collective imagination.

Catholicism asks us to take a broader view. The Church has

outlasted many political and economic systems in the past and is not inclined to see current systems as definitive or permanent. A Catholic worldview, then, is more free to consider the limitations and weaknesses, as well as the strengths, of various political or economic systems than a worldview shaped and perpetuated by those very systems. To take just one example, our public discourse makes it virtually impossible to imagine any other alternative to our current capitalist economy than communism. Even if the Church might prefer capitalism to communism (though this certainly depends on what exactly one means by "capitalism" or "communism"), this theoretical preference can obscure the fact that the Church has serious and legitimate critiques of capitalism as well. Being trapped by the way this question is framed in our culture makes it difficult for many Catholics to hear and appreciate those Catholic thinkers who have taken Catholic Social Teaching seriously and proposed other ways of organizing the economic life of our communities. In the end, both capitalism and communism are essentially materialist worldviews. It is at least odd that Catholics would accept them as the only two real options.

Rather than accepting the false dichotomies and materialist presuppositions inherent in contemporary discourse, Catholicism has its own lenses by which we might look at social questions. Indeed, Scripture insists that humans are, and ought to be, social beings from our very creation: it was not good for Adam to be alone (see Gn 2:18). And part of what it means to be made in the image and likeness of God is to be made for relationship. The doctrine of the Trinity teaches us that God, in himself, is relational. Human beings find their identity and purpose in their relationships with God and with one another.

So, on the one hand, Scripture insists that we are created to live with one another. On the other hand, Scripture is also keenly aware that our social orders can and do perpetuate sin. Cain, who had killed his brother Abel, became the founder of cities. In other words, in our fallen state, our social orders tend to be built on the backs of victims. The people of Israel were keenly aware of this dynamic because they themselves were enslaved by one of history's great empires. Indeed, throughout the Old Testament, Israel is admonished to care for and not to exploit the most vulnerable in their midst — the widow, the orphan, the foreigner — because of their own experience of exploitation in Egypt. Accordingly, Catholic Social Teaching has always highlighted the claims for justice of those left behind by our sinful human systems.

This notion that, like humanity, society is both created good and intended by God, but also fallen and in need of redemption, undergirds all Catholic reflection on social issues. Society is not merely a necessary evil, but neither is it capable of offering us salvation. It is a good in itself, but one compromised by sin. This basic conviction is at the heart of our Catholic engagement with a world that is both beautiful and broken. Moreover, it gives us lenses to recognize the different views of the human person and human society that underlie various political and social proposals, enabling us to engage more critically, creatively, and fruitfully in our own societies. In fact, having access to other categories of thinking about social questions, categories derived from the Church's vision of the human person and developed in Catholic Social Teaching (the dignity of the human person, the common good, solidarity, and subsidiarity) gives Catholics tools to be among the most creative and dynamic participants in the perennial public conversation about how best to organize our common life.

In the rest of this chapter, we'll explore how a Catholic worldview can shed new light on several key questions in contemporary society. A civics or social studies class is often precisely the place where some of the tired and unproductive "cultural default" answers to these questions are given. In a Catholic school, we have the opportunity to offer a healthy corrective; we can better give what rightfully belongs to Caesar when we have first discerned what belongs to God.

THE ROLE OF RELIGION IN SOCIETY

It is not uncommon today for our students to encounter the idea that the role of religion in society is largely negative, that religion's basic social function is that of obstructing progress, whether moral or scientific, and that, the smaller religion's public role, the better. Now, there are certainly examples one can cherry-pick if one wishes to make this case. But the simple fact is that the real impact of religion on society is largely positive and largely invisible. It takes place in soup kitchens and adoption agencies, care homes and hospitals, shelters and crisis pregnancy centers, drop-ins for youth and drop-ins for retirees, parishes and families. It takes place in Catholic schools. And it is not only in these (more or less explicitly) religious contexts, but also in the service that religious people give in society more generally. It is in the upright legislator and the just judge, the kind doctor and the caring counselor, the inspiring teacher and the imaginative artist, the generous neighbor and the loving parent. Millions of these people find the inspiration, wisdom, and strength to live well from their faith.

Given just how widespread negative evaluations of religion's impact on society are today, we should give our students the tools to more accurately appraise that impact. This does not mean making excuses for religions behaving badly. It only means seeing such behavior against the broader background and not using such behavior as the only metric by which we judge religion's contribution to society. Moreover, when making such evaluations it is important to recognize that there are essential differences within "religion" that often get papered over. If the diversity of thought and practice within Islam makes it nonsense to tar every Muslim with the accusation that "Islam is danger-ous," how much less helpful is it to say something as vague as "religion is dangerous"?

It is perfectly possible to find this or that religious idea or practice to be troubling without indicting "religion" as a whole. Indeed, it is more than possible; it is necessary. Harmful ideas and practices should be criticized. Being "religious" should not grant immunity from scrutiny. But saying that religion is dan-gerous because of the harmful ideas of some religious people is like saying politics is dangerous because some politicians have promoted bad policy. The best — in fact, the only — cure for bad religion is better religion.

One of the most important functions of religion in society, before we even get to the question of religious truth, is that of providing our communities with mediating structures between the individual and the state. One of the more distressing features of modern life is the increasingly barren social landscape. The kinds of structures that give us identity and equip us to live as social beings have less and less impact in the lives of many mod-ern people. We are less connected to family, religion, and com-munity and more and more alone in a highly bureaucratized, anonymous, and anonymizing world. It can feel that very little that deeply impacts us happens at a healthy human scale. The resulting felt lack of agency often leads to anxiety and despair, something teachers see in the classroom on a daily basis.

A Catholic vision of a healthy society involves a rich tap-estry of community groups, service clubs, associations related to arts or sport or business, and all manner of humanizing and relational endeavors done with other people. Think of your own students. How does their mental health correlate with their participation in such social groups and activities? And while bowling leagues and bird watching associations are signs of a vital society, two mediating structures stand out as not simply salutary, but essential: families and faith communities. While many mediating structures can and do contribute to a healthier social fabric and better quality of life, family and religion provide the most important buffers against the all-pervasive claims of the state and the market. Only these institutions, which precede the state and form and equip us to live as people with an identity and a set of values that are not given to us by the state, are able to raise up citizens that can genuinely contribute to and thrive in our democracies.

In addition to helping our students make a more just appraisal of religion's role in contemporary society, we also need to help them to understand the role of religion, and of Catholicism in particular, in the development of our culture. Many of the great achievements of western culture are unthinkable without the Church. In various ways, institutions like universities and hospitals, legal principles such as universal human rights, and theoretical breakthroughs like the scientific method can trace their roots to Catholicism. And this is to say nothing of the incomparable contribution the Church has made to art, music, literature, and architecture. Children are going to hear all kinds of things said against the Church as they grow up, only some of it true. In Catholic schools, at least, they should get the whole picture.

CATHOLICISM IN THE PUBLIC SQUARE

One of most important things Catholic schools need to communicate to students is the urgent necessity of their participation in their broader society *as Catholics*. If we are to be the salt of the earth and the light of the world, as Jesus taught, we must engage in our communities as followers of Jesus. This does not mean simply being kind to our neighbors, though that is certainly included. It means serving those in need and advocating for justice in the public sphere. Too often the idea of the separation of Church and State is misused to suggest that religious people should have no voice in the public square. But that was never its intention. This principle was not to protect the public square from religious convictions, but to protect religious convictions from state coercion.

Religious people, like everyone else, are free to bring their convictions and arguments into a vigorous public debate about how to best order our society. And our Catholic schools should prepare our students to do just that. Some might wonder, isn't this "imposing" our beliefs on others? Well, first of all, making a public case is not imposing anything. It is an attempt to persuade and convince. And everyone is allowed, even encouraged, to do that. Second, when it comes time to vote, it is not only religious people trying to impose their beliefs on others; everyone is trying to impose their beliefs on others! That's what voting is. Those voices telling religious people to keep their convictions to themselves seem to have no trouble imposing *their* convictions on society.

Of course, religious people should be aware that, when speaking to a public that does not share their faith commitments, appeals to religious authorities like Scripture or the teaching of the Church may not serve the purpose. There is no reason such appeals should not be *permitted* in public discourse. But being permitted is not the same thing as being *effective*. Catholics have a long tradition of thinking about how to engage with others who do not share all of our convictions. In a Catholic civics or social studies class, the question of how to best engage in a pluralistic public square *as Catholics* should be front and center.

CATHOLICISM AND PLURALISM

Contemporary western societies are probably the most pluralistic societies in the history of the world. Our cities, and not just the metropolises that have always been quite cosmopolitan, but increasingly our mid-size and smaller cities, are bustling with people from every corner of the globe, speaking dozens of languages, and exhibiting a dizzying array of religious and nonreligious perspectives. Such diversity brings energy and excitement, but it also poses important questions. How are we to live well among groups of people so different from one another? What shared values do we need to hold in common to build a healthy society together?

One common answer to these questions is to privatize and relativize religious belief. Religion is divisive, or so we are told. And so, the way for people to live well with others of different religious convictions is to relegate those convictions to the private sphere. Any values that hold us together must not be in any way construed as religious. Under this dispensation, civic values become the only meaningful values, and religion becomes not a search for truth about the deepest questions human beings ask, but a kind of consumer product that may or may not suit a given consumer's needs. The question of religious *truth* is foregone and replaced by the question of religious *utility*. People might believe religious claims because they bring comfort, or resonate with one's cultural identity, or recommend healthy practices to order one's life (or even, let's be honest, because they got hoodwinked by some grifter selling snake oil). But all of that is relative to the needs and desires of that person. It has little to do with what is true.

This version of religion is preferred by many modern people, including some religious folk, who prefer something less demanding, and many nonreligious folk, who prefer something less

threatening. Religion so construed seems far less likely to produce fanaticism than religion that makes genuine truth claims
and asks people to take them seriously. The problem, however, is
that people still want to know and believe true things about the
big questions that have always haunted human beings. People
need to know why their life matters. If religion is so tamed as to
be unable to make any meaningful contribution to these basic
human questions, that does not mean people will stop asking the
questions. It only means that they will look somewhere else for
answers.

In this light, it is not too early to conclude that the strategy
of privatizing and relativizing religion has backfired. It has not
produced less fanaticism, but more. Cutting people off from the
spiritual depths of their religious traditions has created a great
vacuum in our collective search for meaning that is being filled
by everything from ISIS to wokeism to QAnon. Indeed, one of
the more remarkable things about the most extreme elements
in our current political climate — on both sides of the political
spectrum — is their disaffiliation from traditional religion. More
than a few commentators have recognized that this is because
politics has itself come to function as religion. For the most extreme partisans at either end of the spectrum, politics is where
they derive their life's meaning and purpose, where they find
something worth living, and worth dying, for.

As Catholics, we cannot expect to limit religious fanaticism
by watering down our faith. What is needed, rather, is a robust
presentation of the Faith, in all its depth and richness, its beauty and its coherence. This does not, contrary to what much of
contemporary discourse might expect, make us less able to live
well with our neighbors who believe differently. Rather, it allows
us to live honestly with one another. A vigorous but respectful
search for truth among honest neighbors who disagree is a good
and worthy thing. And a pluralism that allows for open and

forthright discussion and debate is a much healthier pluralism than one which imagines that living peaceably together requires ignoring our own deepest convictions and stifling the human search for truth.

Catholicism is well suited to participate in such a healthy pluralism, and even to model a healthy pluralism in the face of an unhealthy one. The Church has, for its part, always insisted that truth is truth wherever it may be found. From the early Church Fathers, who employed the tools of pagan Greek philosophy; to the scholastic theologians like St. Thomas Aquinas, who engaged pagan, Muslim, and Jewish thought; to contemporary thinkers like Thomas Merton, who pursued serious dialogue with the venerable religions of the East, Catholics have always been keen to discern in other religions and worldviews what the Second Vatican Council called "a ray of that Truth which enlightens all men" (*Nostra Aetate*, 2).

PLURALISM AND CATHOLIC SCHOOLS

This tradition of honest and fruitful engagement with the ideas and convictions of those who do not share our faith sets us up well to live among those who believe and think differently than we do. And all of this means that Catholic schools are particularly well suited to form students to live well in a pluralistic society. While much of public education imagines itself to be neutral on questions of religion, what such supposed neutrality most often communicates to students is that religious questions are not important questions. The kind of hollowed-out existence that can follow from being turned away from the pursuit of truth about the questions that matter most — a pursuit that is so natural to us, and to the young in particular — is a spiritual tragedy in itself, even when it does not lead to extremism and fanaticism.

If students learn in a Catholic school to pursue truth with their whole hearts and to engage honestly, charitably, and respectfully with those who do not share their convictions, they will be a blessing to their communities. Moreover, they will be a beacon of hope to those who have been educated out of their natural desire for truth and meaning.

One group that seems to understand this dynamic are those non-Catholic parents who send their children to Catholic schools. They seem to intuit that a Catholic education that teaches things that are quite often opposed to their own religious convictions (be they Evangelical Christians, other Protestants, or even Muslims) is less of a threat to their children's faith than the relativism and "tolerance" on offer in the public schools. They know in their bones, whether or not they can articulate it, that the Catholic insistence that truth matters is preferable to a relativism that construes our deepest convictions as both irrelevant and irrational. They know, that is, what a healthy pluralism looks like.

CATHOLICISM AND DEMOCRACY

One temptation curriculum writers and teachers have is to present democracy through rose-colored glasses, as if the whole political history of the world culminates with democracy and that, now that democracy has been achieved, the only task is to defend it and promote its spread. There are elements of truth in this story, of course. Democracy is much preferable to many other forms of government in human history, and there are certainly elements of democratic societies that deserve our hearty endorsement and vigorous defense. The Catholic concern, however, is with granting any political system the kind of status that makes the establishment and perpetuation of that system an end in itself. Democracy is not the goal; human flourishing is the goal. And democracy is good in so far as it promotes human flourishing.

Moreover, democracy is not without its dangers. Since ancient times, political theorists have been keenly aware of the potential for populism and demagoguery to turn democracy into tyranny. This is why democracies throughout the world have always put checks — such as the Canadian senate or the American electoral college — on "pure" democracy. Now, not every such check works as well as planned, and some, like restricting the franchise to those of a certain race or class or sex, are manifestly unjust. But this should not blind us to the systematic difficulties that come with democracy and the need for checks of some kind. As Catholics, we can reasonably hold both that democracy is, all things considered, a pretty good form of government, and that it is far from perfect. Democracy is something Catholics can work with, and even for, but it is not the Kingdom of God.

Indeed, in recent years, the weaknesses of democracies around the world have been exposed. We are seeing a kind of hyper-partisanship and political polarization that seem so out of control that the very foundations of our political order are threatened. The good news is that the Catholic Tradition, and particularly Catholic teaching on voting and political participation, provides a healthy antidote to this dangerous pattern. The bad news is that the political parties have had such incredible success at colonizing our hearts and minds that many Catholics are more likely to judge their faith through the lens of their political commitments than vice versa.

On both the left and the right, it is easier to find Catholics who will defend or at least excuse their preferred party's unjust policies than to find those who will challenge their own party with the truth of the Gospel. We have basically imported the divisions in our society into the Church itself. And so a huge proportion of the Church's potentially immense political capital is squandered in battles between Catholics who try to justify their own particular political compromises to one another — even to the point of accusing those who make different political compromises of abandoning the Faith — and very little of it is left to challenge the regnant ideologies in the parties themselves. This is nothing less than scandal. In fact, it is idolatry.

In Catholic schools, our students need to learn, first, to judge political policy on the basis of Catholic Social Teaching.* When they do so honestly, they will find that no contemporary political option with any realistic chance of winning an election comports very well with Catholic teaching. This should make clear that any vote is a compromise vote, which is precisely why the Church insists that voting is a matter of prudential judgment, and that good Catholics may well come to different voting decisions in good faith. Moreover, the energy Catholics put into disputing with other Catholics about whom to vote for would be much better spent working for more just policy in their own parties. When we put all our energy into the former, making excuses for our own parties instead of challenging them, we effectively cancel each other out, and the parties don't need to listen to the Catholic witness to truth and justice. Catholic schools can serve an essential role in the healing of our political culture if we can resist the siren song of the parties and form students to prioritize Catholic Social Teaching over partisan politics.

CATHOLICISM AND HUMAN RIGHTS

Contrary to the myth of progress we explored in chapter 6, which imagines that positive modern developments require the jetti-

---

*Every Catholic social studies teacher should own a copy of the Compendium of the Social Doctrine of the Church. Mark Shea's *The Church's Best Kept Secret: A Primer on Catholic Social Teaching* is a very accessible introduction.

soning of our Christian heritage, the concept of human rights is historically rooted in the Christian affirmation of the dignity of every human person, made in the image and likeness of God, and in the natural law tradition of the Catholic Church. While many contemporary secular thinkers strongly affirm a belief in human rights, they do so only on the moral capital of Christianity. Without belief in the inherent dignity of each human person, human rights become easier and easier to dismiss and ignore. Indeed, we can expect to see increasing attacks on the classical concept of human rights as the western world becomes more and more detached from its Christian roots. It is a testament to the power of the Christian ideal, however, that even such attacks are often made in the name of human rights.

And so, our students should learn of the explicitly Christian development of the idea of human rights. One salient historical example is the work of Bartolomé de las Casas, whose defense of the Indigenous population of the Caribbean against the exploitation of their Spanish conquerors was a signal development toward the modern concept of human rights. De las Casas was deeply rooted in the thought of St. Thomas Aquinas, which gave him the perspective to challenge the predominant voices of his own day. Students should also learn of the specifically Christian motivations and arguments of great champions of human rights, such as William Wilberforce, who worked tirelessly for the elimination of slavery in the British Empire, and Martin Luther King Jr., who referenced St. Thomas Aquinas in his famous "Letter from Birmingham Jail." They should know about the explicitly Christian history — including the contribution of Catholic philosopher Jacques Maritain — of the United Nations Universal Declaration on Human Rights in 1948.

But we also need to recognize the ways in which rights language, as it drifts further and further away from its Christian origins, is increasingly co-opted as a political tool that is weaponized in the culture wars. To take just one example, it would have been unimaginable to those who developed and promoted the concept of human rights that some future notion of "reproductive rights" would one day pit the rights of mothers against those of their unborn children. As a coherent whole, human rights were meant to affirm the dignity of every human person. But in their piecemeal application in the culture wars, they often become just one more way for one group to assert power over another. We should be wary, then, of the indiscriminate use of rights language in ways that ignore our responsibilities to one another and turn us into ever more isolated individuals whose relationship with the broader community is limited to getting "my due."

CATHOLICISM, POPULATION, AND THE ENVIRONMENT

To blame population growth instead of extreme and selective consumerism on the part of some, is one way of refusing to face the issues.

POPE FRANCIS

In the early 1990s, my grade 9 social studies classroom had a chart on the wall that presented the dramatic explosion of the human population in the twentieth century and extrapolated it into the future in a way that made global population growth look like a runaway train. My classmates and I were fascinated — and terrified. It looked like simple math that the world was going to run out of room, and fast. The notion of an overcrowded planet is still widespread today. But is it true?

In fact, already by the time the map in my classroom was

produced, the growth rate of the human population was in serious decline. And it is basically assured that most of the students in today's classrooms will live to see global population peak and then begin to fall, probably precipitously. Several nations, like Japan and Russia, are already there. Many other countries are only avoiding population decline by relying on immigration. But the birth rates in the countries of origin for those immigrants are also dropping rapidly. Immigration is a temporary solution at best.

In the not-very-far-off future, we will be struggling with major challenges related to population decline. The most obvious difficulty is trying to pay for social programs with a shrinking workforce and tax base. This is why governments all over the world have been experimenting with policies to boost their national birth rates (just google "Do it for Denmark!") for a generation now, though with little success. But there are other difficulties as well. Advances in research and technology, for instance, are typically a function of population. When every hand is needed just to meet society's basic needs, no one has time to build rockets or develop antibiotics.

And the social costs are enormous. Have you ever considered that China's now abandoned one-child policy meant that, within one generation of no brothers and sisters, there would be no such things as aunts, uncles, or cousins? Meanwhile, Japan is pioneering robots to keep the elderly company while they die alone. And still, many of our young people have got the impression that having a child is an irresponsible thing to do. Some have even sworn off having a family altogether. This is a recipe for heartache for individuals, and economic and social disaster for nations.

In a Catholic school, part of teaching the dignity of every human person is the emphatic rejection of the view that humans are basically parasites on nature and that having children contributes to the destruction of the planet. Rather, we should learn that one of the best things we can do for our world is to bring children into a loving family and raise them to fulfill God's mission for their lives. Human beings are not simply consumers, a horde of locusts devouring the resources of a finite planet. We are stewards of creation, contributing, building, even midwifing to birth the stunning potential God built into the universe.

But what does this mean for our Christian duty to care for creation? Is the human population not a great threat to the health of the planet? We absolutely have a duty to care for our planet, and the urgency of that duty is clearer today than ever before. But we are right to challenge the straightforward assertion that the basic problem is the raw number of people. It is clear that we will soon face the difficulties, not of overpopulation, but of underpopulation. And if it leads to technological stagnation, cutting off promising developments in areas such as clean energy and food production, underpopulation may itself have undesirable consequences for the environment. Which is to say nothing of the potential losses in terms of quality of life. The people who are going to defeat cancer need to be born first. But the issue is more complicated than even that.

While it is easy to find talking heads who claim without evidence things like "The earth's carrying capacity is 1 billion people; we're already 7 billion people over capacity," the fact is that it makes no sense to claim some specific finite number as the earth's carrying capacity without reference to consumption. If everyone lived the lifestyle of the western elite, with private jets and second and third homes, the planet would collapse in short order. On the other hand, even in highly industrialized nations like Canada and the United States there are people who manage to live a net zero — or better! — lifestyle. In other words, fretting about population, which is set to decline in any case, is largely a distraction from the real issue — namely, out-of-control consumption. How just is it for those of us whose consumption is most conspicuous to concern ourselves with lowering birth rates in Africa, where most people use a tiny fraction of the resources we do?

Assignment Idea: Research and Presentation

Each of the following could be a research assignment leading to a class presentation.

Food waste: What percentage of the world's food requirement do we produce? What percentage of that is wasted? How and where is it wasted? What is the carbon footprint (fertilizer, shipping, refrigeration) of the food that never gets eaten? What are some innovative ways we can cut down on food waste as individuals and as societies?

Consumption inequality: Compare the amount of resources used by average citizens of various countries. Compare the amount of resources used by different segments of the population within the same country. What is the relative contribution of various lifestyle decisions — for example, vacations requiring flights, eating meat every day, having far more clothes than I need, etc. — to my carbon footprint? What are the simplest, most effective ways to reduce the impact of my own consumption patterns?

Living net zero: Find examples of people living a net zero (or better) lifestyle in various environments. How do they do it? Is their lifestyle replicable? Scalable? How? How not?

Green technology: Which technologies offer the most promise toward helping the environment? Are they likely to be adopted? What barriers do they face? Who developed them? Why? How?

Demographics: What is the current growth rate of the global human population? How is that rate changing? When will the human population go into decline? What are some of the social and economic consequences of population decline in countries where this is already a reality? How can we best mitigate population decline?

KEY TAKEAWAYS

A Catholic education pushes back against the absolutization of politics and economics and, rooted in Catholic Social Teaching, imagines possibilities beyond contemporary political and economic models.

In a Catholic school, students should get an honest and balanced assessment of the role of religion, and of Catholicism in particular, in society.

Catholic schools should form students to participate in public life *as Catholics*. Healthy pluralism does not require a watering down of religious conviction, but a common commitment to pursue truth together.

A Catholic education must not import our political divisions into the Church, but rather equip students to bring healing and unity to our political culture.

A Catholic approach to population and the environment insists that fears about overpopulation are in fact a distraction from the real concern: overconsumption.

Chapter 10
Health

Health class is not only about diseases, nutrition, and exercise. It also includes a focus on things like peer pressure, relationships, family, and mental health. Health class deals with the whole human person. Catholics can certainly endorse such a holistic approach. We are not only physical beings, and ignoring basic elements of our humanity through a narrow focus on the physical does not lead to human flourishing. Indeed, it is now commonly accepted and empirically verified that spiritual care is an essential part of health care for just this reason.

On the other hand, the fact that we are dealing with the whole person means that it is very easy for non-Catholic attitudes towards the human person to slip into our health classes unnoticed. If we are not explicitly Catholic in our treatment of the whole person in health class, all kinds of cultural assumptions about what constitutes human flourishing will happily assert themselves. And most students will never imagine these assumptions are anything but neutral — just the way things are.

Because of this, health class poses a particular challenge when it deals with questions related to morality, such as sexuality or death and dying, because the supposedly "neutral" approach to such matters in health class can make it seem that what is being taught down the hall in religion class is, at best, arbitrary and disconnected from reality, and, at worst, counterproductive or even dangerous. This experience can make religion seem less and less relevant to students. When what health class teaches is perceived to be in conflict with what religion class teaches, it is the rare student who will opt for religion. And even that rare student will be saddled with the false impression that being a good Catholic means ignoring, downplaying, or even opposing what we know from other disciplines, instead of integrating all knowledge within a cohesive Catholic framework. This is often a first step on the way to a "privatized" and innocuous faith, even if it keeps the trappings of Catholic piety.

SEX AND RELATIONSHIPS

Because it is an area where the differences between a Catholic approach and the surrounding culture are so obvious and contentious, it would be easy to let a discussion of sex and relationships dominate this chapter. That said, the very fact of this tension means there are already many resources for Catholic teachers on this question. In fact, I wrote *How Far Can We Go? A Catholic Guide to Sex and Dating* (with my friend Leah Perrault) on just this topic. In it, Leah and I not only do our best to give a credible and accurate account of Church teaching on human sexuality, but to give very practical advice about developing healthy relationships that help young people better understand themselves and others.

I hope that teachers will find much in it of value for their work.

For the purposes of this chapter, allow me to simply note that there is a danger that the framework through which sex is approached in health class is basically one of risk management. It is easy to unwittingly communicate that sex is a kind of physical need, even a right, that people have, and that the most important thing is that they meet that need safely. This leads to a kind of confusion wherein sex is simultaneously very important — a basic biological need like food and water — and not very important at all — because it does not actually *mean* anything and can be done with almost anyone for almost any reason.

This leads to unsettling conclusions. Several years ago, a popular Canadian radio host was credibly accused of battering women during sexual encounters. The public discussion that followed was remarkable for what it did *not* say. While it led to important conversations about consent, no one dared ask if there was anything actually wrong with violence against women during sex, or with a person who found such violence sexually exciting. Because there was no common understanding of the *meaning* of sex in Canadian society (as, for example, a gift for sharing love and life in a lifelong, vowed, committed relationship open to children), sex was reduced to what consenting adults might choose to do for mutual pleasure. When that is the measure, the notion that they might choose something morally wrong becomes simply unintelligible. And so, a man physically assaulting a woman, something that almost everyone considers immoral in any other context, became just something that some folks like to do in their spare time.

In a Catholic health class, it is important not to contradict Church teaching on questions of the morality of certain acts. We also need to convey a picture of the beauty and meaning of human sexuality wherein Church teaching can actually make sense. Consent is absolutely necessary for a healthy and rightly ordered sexuality, but it is far from sufficient. If we talk about safety or consent as if they are the only categories for understanding sex, and do not seek to integrate these notions into a Catholic vision of the meaning of marriage and sexuality, we undermine what is being taught down the hall in religion class and set our students up for heartache.

SUFFERING

I suffered a lot but my soul was singing! I have nothing left, but I still have my heart and with that I can always love.

BLESSED CHIARA LUCE BADANO

The un-Catholic idea that might sneak most easily into health class is the contemporary elevation of health as, perhaps, the highest good. Think about what people often say to new parents immediately after asking if the child is a girl or a boy. Some version of, "Well, it doesn't matter, as long as they're healthy." Now, this is certainly well intentioned, and it even carries an important truth. Neither boys nor girls are better than the other, and health *is* better than illness. We are right to wish health for our children and for all children. But often buried underneath this truth is the notion, perhaps only partially and unconsciously believed, that a life of someone suffering with illness is worth less than other lives. Consider how this well-meaning phrase — "as long as they're healthy" — might sound *to you* if *your child* is not, in fact, healthy?

Joseph Ratzinger once wrote, "A worldview that is incapable of giving even pain meaning and value is good for nothing." A health class that teaches students how to live well and pursue health is good. But a health class that gives the impression that it is impossible to live well without health is dangerous. Because everyone gets sick. And everyone dies.

In our culture, we are usually taught to think of the disabled as a separate and discrete category of people — a "minority" — but the fact is that most of us will be disabled at some point or other. If we remember that people are often disabled by mental illness, and not only by things like accidents and degenerative diseases, or that disability does not need to be permanent to be real, or that we all just slowly lose ability as we age, this becomes obvious. Disability, suffering, pain, illness, and death are nonnegotiables. If we cannot live well with these realities, we cannot live well, period.

Health is a great good, but it is a terrible god. Health should be genuine priority in our lives, but if it becomes a god, if we sacrifice everything for the sake of it, we will be let down as with any false god. If it becomes our highest good, it will demand virtually unlimited sacrifices. But there is no sacrifice we can make to this god that will protect us from the inevitable. No one gets out of here alive.

ASSISTED SUICIDE

Because we are unable to face the ultimate pain of our life and the reality of our death, and to look suffering in the eye, we have come to believe that a painless existence, a healthy life, is the highest good on earth.

ULRICH LEHNER

In an ironic twist, worshipping health and delaying death at all costs has contributed to our cultural drift toward assisted suicide. Worshipping health relies on and contributes to the lie that suffering makes life meaningless. Then, faced with the inevitability of suffering and death, we have no resources to live well with our frail human condition, and opting out looks very appealing. Far from relieving suffering, this "solution" actually multiplies it. Instead of relieving people from being a burden on their families and societies, it practically *accuses* them of being a burden. Instead of building the networks of care that grow around the suffering and dying, networks that so often heal and sustain our families and communities, assisted suicide nips such networks in the bud.

And what is the more and more obvious solution for suffering people who feel themselves to be ever more burdensome, in a culture with weaker and weaker social networks? Assisted suicide is always promoted as a solution for extreme, heart-wrenching cases, but it introduces a logic that guarantees more and more of the suffering for which it is the supposed solution. To work to limit suffering is noble. But to imagine we can be rid of suffering is delusional. And that delusion ends up sustaining itself by getting rid of sufferers. When I say that false gods demand sacrifices, I am not speaking metaphorically.

So, one thing that a Catholic health class needs to incorporate is the idea of living well with illness. Not every illness can be healed. People, maybe most people, live with chronic conditions, physically and mentally. Students need to see examples of people, from canonized saints to folks in their own communities, who have learned to live well with suffering. More than that, they should be introduced to the spiritual riches of the Church that have helped millions to live well with illness. We worship a God who became one of us and suffered and died and rose again. And we are offered the possibility of joining our suffering with his, turning our lives and deaths into a gift as Jesus did. Suffering is not meaningless. And death does not have the final word. It is through suffering that God has saved and is saving the world. Our God is always turning death to new life. If students graduate from Catholic schools and this is their one key takeaway from health class, we will have prepared them to live — and to die — well.

We should notice, however, that there is a real danger that this kind of theological language can be used as a cop-out by those who are uncomfortable *being with sufferers*. It is easier to ignore people's suffering and offer them cheap advice — for example, "everything happens for a reason" — than to hear and acknowledge their pain. That God can redeem suffering should be our invitation to join with others' pain, not to dismiss it.

Though evil is never good, God can bring good out of evil. Many people have learned virtue through suffering. Most readers of this book will be able to reflect on the illness or death of a loved one that was morally inspiring. My own brother died of brain cancer when he was twenty-four years old. At his funeral, we read from an Old Testament passage that spoke of "being perfected in a short time" (Wis 4:13). It rang true. While illness transformed his body for the worse, it transformed his soul for the better. We had all seen it with our own eyes.

If Christianity offers us hope beyond death, it certainly offers us hope beyond illness. In health class we have an opportunity to wrestle with some of the biggest questions humans ask: questions about suffering and death and meaning and goodness in the face of evil. And Catholicism gives us unsurpassed tools for just this kind of work. What a lost opportunity if health class in a Catholic school is indistinguishable from health class anywhere else!

SPIRITUALITY

To be human is to be spiritual. People are going to wrestle with the big questions and problems of life some way or another. (Even burying things in our subconscious is a way, if not a very good one, of dealing with these things.) We all figure out ways — better or worse, conscious or unconscious — to deal with life's biggest questions and problems, and this helps us understand what "spirituality" actually means.

We often imagine that being "spiritual" means being interested in spiritual things, like church or prayer, or believing in the supernatural. A so-called spiritual person might be religious and into "churchy" things. Or she might do her spiritual stuff outside of the context of organized religion. Sometimes we even use the word "spiritual" to describe people, conventionally religious or not, who are really just superstitious.

This is all based on a misunderstanding, namely, that being spiritual is a kind of lifestyle choice or personality trait. Something some folks enjoy and others don't. Nonsense! Spirituality is not a penchant for certain kinds of practices or ideas; it is the way that humans try to make sense of their world. We are meaning makers. To ask a question is a spiritual act. To understand another person is a spiritual act. To judge something beautiful is a spiritual act. To believe that something is true is a spiritual act.

We are not content with merely meeting our physical needs. The fact that we have needs beyond things like food, air, water, or shelter means that we are spiritual beings. If we need belonging, identity, compassion, meaning, purpose, and value, we are spiritual. If we can consider the difference between right and wrong, we are spiritual. If we worship (and we all do, one way or another), we are spiritual. The spiritual is the realm of meaning, and humans will pursue meaning to the point that they neglect or even renounce their physical needs to get it.

Spirituality, then, is nothing more (and nothing less!) than the set of beliefs and practices that we all engage in to make sense of our world and to try and live in a way that makes sense to us. Every human person has a spirituality. It may well be one that is not up to the task, but a poor spirituality is no less a spirituality than an unhealthy diet is a diet. Even addiction can be a kind of spirituality — or perhaps the outworking of a spirituality. If we believe lies about our own intrinsic worth and undertake practices to numb the resulting pain in our hearts, addiction often results. The "drinking saltwater" logic of addiction is emblematic of many of our deepest spiritual struggles. When we are in pain, we often return to the very thing that is hurting us.

The only way out of destructive spirituality is healthy spirituality. We need true beliefs to counter the destructive lies we have believed, and we need healthy practices to deal with the struggles of life in a way that does not simply avoid them in the present by pushing them into the future. Catholicism has a great treasury of spirituality that is eminently practical. As Catholic health teachers, we need to familiarize ourselves with the spiritual resources in our own tradition.

These spiritual resources can be a great blessing to us and to our students as we learn to navigate the difficulties of life. But let me offer one caution. Many people have had real struggles with mental illness dismissed or poorly handled by people in the Church who treated mental illness as essentially a spiritual problem that could be appropriately managed through prayer alone. Make no mistake, prayer is essential for all our struggles, mental illness included. But mental illness also requires treatment by a qualified professional. To suggest that such help is unnecessary because of the power of prayer is dangerous. Not only might it keep someone from getting the treatment they need, it can create an additional burden of guilt when the prayer "doesn't work."

Now, don't imagine that I am asking you to downplay Christian teaching about prayer. Quite the contrary! It is the false notion that prayer is really about getting what we think is best for us if we only ask God with enough faith that is the real downplaying of Christian teaching. If prayer were simply about getting what we want, Jesus never would have died on the cross after his prayer in the Garden of Gethsemane.

God answers every prayer. Sometimes the answer is "yes," but sometimes it is "no." Sometimes it is "wait and see." Maybe the most common answer God gives to prayer, if we take the time to listen for an answer, is something like, "Are you sure about that?" If what the Gospels tell us about Jesus is any indication, it is not out of character for God to answer a question with a question. Simply introducing the possibility of waiting for God's response and the notion that God's answers can go beyond "yes" or "no" can transform an underdeveloped prayer life. What kinds of outcomes proper to a health class might be met if students had a prayer journal where they recorded not only their prayers, but what happened when they stopped to listen for God's answers?

Christian prayer ends with "Amen," which means something like "Thy will be done." Prayer is much more about learning to see things from God's point of view than about getting what we want or think we need. We should still ask for what we think we need in prayer. But that is largely because honestly putting those requests before the Lord gives God the chance to teach us what we really need, not because God is a kind of gumball machine that pays out if you put in the right coins — or worse, a slot machine that pays out unpredictably, but just enough to keep you on the hook hoping for the big one. Prayer is how we learn to see everything, even our own suffering, through the loving eyes of God.

VIRTUE

As we explored in Chapter 1, the truly happy person is not the one who has every need met right now, on demand. Indeed, what kind of person might you become if you never had to struggle for anything, if everything was handed to you on a platter as soon as you asked? We do not do this for our own children, and for good reason. Why would God do it with us? No, the truly happy person is the person who is freed from needing to have every want addressed in the moment. If our happiness depends on life going exactly as we desire or imagine, we will be miserable. We need internal resources, because external rewards will come and go. That is why the truly happy person is the virtuous person.

Health class is the ideal context in which to present Catholic teaching about virtue to our students. Growth in virtue is intimately related to what we have defined as "spirituality" in this chapter. A healthy spirituality leads to growth in virtue, and an unhealthy spirituality leads to vice. No one makes decisions about food, exercise, sex, friends, social media, work, or anything else that might be explored in health class without reference to their own spirituality — their basic set of beliefs and practices for making sense of the world. Nor could they.

Let's take one of our most basic needs as an example. The *human* question about food is not, as we might naïvely imagine, "What will I eat?" but "How do I make meaning out of what I eat?" And so, anyone trying to influence behavior, for good or ill, must tap into the spiritual — the realm of meaning. Advertisers know this. Think of the last billboard you saw for food. (This might make a good assignment in a Catholic health class!) What meaning was it trying to communicate? Did it appeal to your sense of yourself as someone who is responsible and health-conscious? As someone who deserves a treat? As someone who buys ethically? As someone whose time is valuable? As someone on a budget? Advertisers know that if they want to sell things to humans, they need to appeal to *meaning*.

Or consider diet plans. It is virtually impossible to change your basic eating patterns without changing the way you make meaning with food. Willpower can rarely keep a person on track for more than twenty-four hours or so. What is needed is a new way of looking at food and its relationship to one's life and, very often, a community to reinforce and support that point of view. Or think about how some gyms or exercise regimes brand themselves as quasi-religious. They might be being cheeky, but it's funny because it's true. They, too, are invested in human meaning making.

WHO MAKES YOUR MEANING?

We are constantly buffeted by outside interests who are trying to make our meaning for us in order to manipulate our behavior. This has always been true to some degree, but it is true in a unique way for hyper-consumerist late modernity, where "consumer" can easily become our primary identity, and where we carry the meaning makers in our pockets. Earlier generations worried about letting the meaning makers into our living rooms. Now we take them with us to bed and to the toilet.

In this context, a healthy spirituality is both more difficult and more necessary. The person who knows who she is and what she believes, and has built habits to live in accordance with that knowledge and belief, is well-equipped to deal with the partial, the biased, and even the straight-up false meaning making that assails us every waking moment. But it is hard to be the people we want to be when we are constantly bombarded with external images and ideas. Indeed, it can be hard even to know what kind of people we want to be if we never spend time alone with our thoughts.

A recent study, discussed in R. J. Snell's article titled "Education and the Restoration of Moral Agency," found that fully one-third of young people could not answer a question about what made something right or wrong. Several seemed not to even understand the question. The explanation for such a finding surely includes many factors, but it is probable that one of these is that we fill every spare minute with our devices. A distracted population does not know how to think about deep questions.

Which brings us to perhaps the single biggest health issue facing young people today. Social media is a kind of perfect culmination of consumerism. Through it, even the consumer becomes a product. A strange inversion takes place whereby we — our time, our attention, our data — are now what is for sale. More than that, we are trained by the platforms themselves to think of ourselves as products. We must satisfy our audiences, and so we curate our profiles accordingly, whether that means taking thousands of selfies in order to find the right one, or virtue signaling by liking all the right posts about social issues without ever having to do any real work for justice in our communities. To post the wrong pic or the wrong opinion can be socially and emotionally devastating. Our own meaning making is easily hijacked by algorithms that make our meaning for us based on what will keep our eyes on the screen. We do not only lose our time on social media; if we are not careful, we can lose ourselves.

Faced with such a challenge, we need serious spiritual resources. Fasting, often imagined as an arbitrary rule imposed on Catholics by an authoritarian Church, deserves a second look. Jesus himself taught that the worst demons could only be driven out with prayer and fasting. Fasting is meaning making with food! And it can mean a few distinct but related things. Fasting can be a practice to improve one's health and relationship with food, an awareness-raising solidarity with those who do not have enough to eat, or a form of self-discipline. Underneath each of these is the spiritual reality that taking a break allows us to see our lives with more clarity. The same logic underlies an hour of meditation before the Blessed Sacrament, going on retreat, or practicing Sabbath by not working or shopping on Sunday (i.e., meaning making with work and consumption). All these practices give us a kind of critical distance from our everyday patterns so that we might consider them anew and ask ourselves if the way we live really does align with our highest goals and truest beliefs.

And we can fast from things other than food. If there is one thing that social media companies and the advertisers they serve fear, it is consumers who recharge their sense of freedom and self-possession by taking intentional, even rigid, breaks from their devices. There might be no more impactful fast for your students (and maybe for yourself!) than a strict no-devices-in-the-bedroom rule. Indeed, an assignment that asked students to turn off their phones between 8:30 p.m. and 8:30 a.m. and leave them on the kitchen counter overnight for a week or two, and then to reflect on the impact of that practice on their health — mental, emotional, physical, and spiritual — could be life-changing. It should at least prove enlightening. This could easily be layered with other practices, like prayer or exercise or visiting a loved one, over the course of a semester. Such practices build good habits, and good habits become virtues, and virtues make it easier to live well each day. Change your habits; change your life.

SACRAMENTS: GOD'S MEANING MAKERS

It is easy for contemporary people to imagine that the appropriate response to the meaning making done on our behalf by the corporations and social media platforms that dominate our lives and imaginations is a kind of self-assertion. We think that we can find some true self apart from any external social influence and take a stand. This is naïve. The "self" that emerges here, expressed in things as diverse as radical political ideologies, novel gender constructs, or conspiracy theories — all of which portray themselves as rebelling against some radically compromised "mainstream" — is at least as open to manipulation as any other construction of self. Those who imagine themselves to be the most independent thinkers are often hopelessly dependent on unscrupulous meaning making profiteers, whether those are found on the dark web or in the academy.

Human meaning making is inherently communal. There is no "true self" outside external influence. The question is, which external influence is determinative? Who gets to say who we are and what our value is? God. God does.

And that is good news! Consider: Are you most yourself after spending an hour scrolling social media or an hour before the Blessed Sacrament? If you're not sure, do a test. Take a week where you dedicate a specific time to quiet prayer with the Eucharist, and then spend that same time slot the next week on social media and observe your inner life through a practice like journaling. Perhaps you could make some variation of this into an assignment for your health class?

Because God created us, God gets to say who we really are. And he has. He has told us that we are beloved sons and daughters. Think about the competition in meaning making that goes on with the Sacrament of Reconciliation. If you're like me, you have gone to reconciliation dozens and dozens of times, and you still kind of dread it. Every time, I fret about revealing myself to the priest as a sinner. And every time, I walk out shining. Why is this? In this sacrament, my own meaning making about my sin, my temptation to reduce my own identity to my failures, is overruled when God — immediately after hearing about those very failures! — reassures me that my identity is grounded in God's love for me and not in my brokenness. We interpret sin as who we are, but God says: "Sin is not who you are. Sin is your enemy, and I release you from your fear and bondage to this enemy. You are free!"

Deep down, we do not really want to be the final arbiters of meaning in our lives. We are creatures, and sinful ones at that, not God. Our meaning making is an attempt to see reality clearly. Sometimes we do better at this and sometimes we do worse. But God's meaning making determines reality itself. When God creates us, we are created; when God forgives us, we are forgiven. And it is good news when God's meaning making corrects the flaws in our own. In God's forgiveness, we rejoice to find we were mistaken. In baptism, God calls us into his own family, and so we truly are God's family. At Mass, God feeds us with his own Body, and so we become his Body. If we want to find our true selves and our true meaning, we need to go to the source of our being, which is not ourselves, but our loving God.

Assignment Idea: Fasting

Fasting gives us critical distance from our habits so that we can consider whether the way we are living really does support the person we want to be. Make an assignment where students give up something, perhaps replacing it with something else, and then reflect on how that change impacts their lives. Probably the most impactful fast for most students today will be from their phones. So, have students spend a week with no phone access between 8:30 p.m. and 8:30 a.m. Or have them go two or three days with no phone access at all. There can be lots of choice and variation built into such an assignment. The point is to make a concrete change and reflect on its impact, perhaps by journaling. What do I learn about myself by this practice? And what might I want to change about my habits going forward? Various combinations and layers of habits (both giving up old ones and starting new ones) can be combined. What if, instead of watching TV for a week, I go for a walk during the time I usually watch TV? This does not mean phones or TV are bad. It means they often unconsciously take over our lives without our willing it. Fasting can make our life habits more intentional.

KEY TAKEAWAYS

Because health class (rightly) deals with the whole human person, certain cultural assumptions about human flourishing can easily sneak in. Catholic health teachers need to have a clear Catholic vision of human flourishing.

In a Catholic health class, we must not reduce the question of sex to issues of safety and consent. Rather, we need a picture of the meaning and beauty of the gift of sexuality.

In a Catholic health class, we have the resources of our whole tradition to deal with questions of human suffering. We must counter the dangerous idea that suffering makes a good and valuable life impossible.

If spirituality is about beliefs and practices to make sense of life, there are many outcomes proper to a health class that can be met by exploring spirituality in health class. Our Catholic tradition gives us great resources in this regard.

Our decisions are rooted in how we make sense of the world. But, on top of our own flaws, our meaning making is strongly influenced by powers that do not have our best interests at heart. Fasting can be a way to find some freedom from these meaning makers. And the sacraments can be understood as God's antidote to so much of the false meaning making we encounter.

Chapter 11
School Sports and Physical Education

Did you know that the presence of physical education and sports in schools has Catholic roots? St. Thomas Aquinas argued that it was against the virtue of moderation to work all the time, and that well-rounded, healthy, virtuous people make time for play and recreation. Later educators, including the Jesuits, referred to this argument when introducing sport and play into the school day.

Indeed, this is far from the only Catholic argument in favor of physical education. A Catholic anthropology insists that God created us body and soul and that this is, like everything else God created, good. More than that, in Jesus, God became one of us, taking on a human body. It is difficult to imagine a stronger statement on the goodness of the body than that. Unfortunately, throughout Church history, some Christians have been tempted by the non-Christian idea that, while spirit is good, matter is bad. This is often referred to as "Gnosticism," though, properly speaking, this was only one aspect of actual Gnosticism. This worldview, which threatened orthodox Christian belief at several points, was common in the ancient world and shows up in various guises throughout Church history. Many have noted that modern versions of it are behind various cultural movements today that deny the goodness of the body or treat the true self as having no real connection to our God- given bodies.

Even within Christian circles, the presumption that matter is bad can lead to the belief that our souls are our true selves and our bodies are simply the imperfect shells those souls inhabit during this earthly life. This is actually a serious distortion of Christian teaching. We believe in the *resurrection of the body*. We don't just *have* bodies; we *are* our bodies. And we will not be fully ourselves with God and the angels and saints forever in heaven until we have been reunited with our bodies, which God created good and which he will raise on the last day.

BODY AND SOUL

The Church considers sports as an instrument of education when they foster high human and spiritual ideals and when they form young people in an integral way to develop in such values as loyalty, perseverance, friendship, solidarity and peace.

POPE ST. JOHN PAUL II

A genuine Catholic worldview does not denigrate the body, but honors it, as Saint Paul teaches, as a temple of the Holy Spirit.

Moreover, the relationship between body and soul gives rise to the whole, complex human person, who must be engaged spiritually, emotionally, intellectually, socially, *and* physically. This is true of how we are engaged in the liturgy of the Church. It is true of how any healthy human relationship works. And it is true of Catholic education. If the body is ignored or downplayed, then we are failing to educate the whole person.

Thus, Catholic education has always understood that sports and physical education are key to developing the emotional, social, intellectual, and spiritual facets of our humanity *through* our engagement with the physical. Consider that when we watch the Olympics, we do not hear of "the triumph of the human body." Instead, even our secular world recognizes, in the stunning athletic achievements on display at the Olympics, "the triumph of the human spirit." As Pope St. John Paul II once said: "Athletic activity, in fact, highlights not only man's valuable physical abilities, but also his intellectual and spiritual capacities. ... It also has a soul and must show its complete face."

This integration of the physical and the spiritual, of body and soul, means that, while other areas of study, like music or literature, may lend themselves more than others to including Catholic *content*, there may be no place in our Catholic schools as ready-made to highlight a Catholic *context* as physical education and school sports. In addition to the affirmation of the goodness of the body that must undergird all our efforts in this area, sports and exercise provide a uniquely challenging and fruitful context for developing virtue. The discipline of hard work, the cooperation with a team, the character needed to win or lose well, the courage to compete against long odds — sport fosters all of these. More than that, understood through the Catholic lens, sport can even be an antidote to many currents of thought and ideologies in contemporary society that hamper the cultivation of virtues and the development of the whole person. On the other hand, precisely because it touches so deeply on questions of human formation, there are also cautions to be observed regarding our attitudes toward sport. Let's explore these ideas in more depth, beginning with competitive sports.

FOSTERING VIRTUE

This is the logic of sport, especially Olympic sports; it is also the logic of life: without sacrifices, important results are not obtained, or even genuine satisfaction.

POPE ST. JOHN PAUL II

Faithful and virtuous coaches who hold their teams and athletes to high standards — athletic and moral — can often be the most effective transmitters of Catholic values on a school's staff. High school-age students in particular are at a critical time of life when they need both respected role models and clear boundaries. This is also the time of life when adult mentors from outside the immediate family become more important as children develop their sense of themselves and their relationship to the wider world. How many good coaches have filled this role over the years?

The good coach knows that sports have an incredible capacity to teach us about life. Indeed, one reason we humans love not just to play sports, but to watch them, or why sports themes make for so many great movies, is precisely because sports are always a metaphor for life. Saint Paul knew this when he chose images from sport — running the race, fighting the fight — as analogies for the Christian life. We might even imagine competitive sports as a kind of concentrated microcosm of life, where the consequences of our every action and decision are brought before us with unavoidable and undeniable clarity. Is there a better exercise in honesty and humility than watching and analyzing one's mistakes on film the day after a loss? Even if a mistake is not necessarily the same thing as a sin, this is a striking analogy for understanding the examination of conscience before the Sacrament of Penance; both require an unflinching look at my reality accompanied by a genuine commitment to improve, to do whatever is within my power to be my best.

The disciplines required by competitive sports — practicing diligently, going to bed on time and getting up early, eating well and exercising — help to mature students into responsible and competent adults. Through them, young people learn that a fulfilling and satisfying life requires giving up lower goods for higher ones — that goals have costs. Indeed, in this, sports teach what Christianity teaches: Sacrifice is the way to the good life.

Learning to work as part of a team is also great practice for life. Whether in our families, our workplaces, our churches, or our civic communities, we need to be able to commit to one another, work towards shared goals, cooperate, recognize and balance one another's strengths and weaknesses, and support and encourage one another. We also need to learn how to discern what we are responsible for and what we are not. There is a healthy way in which we are responsible for one another, and an unhealthy way in which we are tempted to take ownership of things beyond our control. The first leads to solidarity. The second leads to poor boundaries, anxiety, and burnout. A good coach understands this almost intuitively and shapes a team's culture accordingly. Being on such a team can be one of the most formative experiences in a young person's life.

Approached the right way, sports teach us that we have agency and responsibility — that our efforts make a real difference to the outcome we pursue — *and* that our agency has limits. Once we have done our best, we must learn to accept outcomes we would not choose for ourselves. Every athlete knows the difference between the feeling that follows a loss where both teams played their hearts out and one of them had to lose, and the feeling that follows a loss where one's own team was lazy, arrogant, unfocused, or undisciplined. The first is unavoidable. Sad, yes, but tinged with the joy and satisfaction that comes from knowing you did all you could. The feeling after a loss where you did not give your best is much worse.

A good coach knows that a loss is a great opportunity for growth and the development of character. A good coach accepts no excuses, gives credit where credit is due, and expects athletes to do the same. Yes, bad luck, like an injury or a one-in-a-million bounce, can be a factor. But here, too, there is opportunity for learning. We are only responsible for what we are responsible for. Did we do everything we could to succeed? That is the question that matters. In life, like in sports, you can only do your best. Every person needs to learn that there are outcomes beyond our control. The person who can only be happy when everything goes their way will never be happy.

RECREATIONAL SPORTS

I entertain a private suspicion that physical sports were much more really effective and beneficent when they were not taken quite so seriously. One of the first essentials of sport being healthy is that it should be delightful; it is rapidly becoming a false religion with austerities and prostrations.

G. K. CHESTERTON

While it is certainly true that competitive sports offer a unique opportunity for the development of many virtues, we must be careful to avoid giving the impression that sports only have value if one is good enough to play them at a competitive level. In most schools, only a minority of students will be on the school teams. And only a minority of those will be really good. The reality is that all students need to learn the lessons of sport. Physical education class should not just be for jocks.

Sports at a less competitive level can be a wonderful part of a healthy and fulfilling life. The same virtues we have explored above can be developed here too, if not always with the same intensity. Simply attending to one's physical and mental health through exercise can make a dramatic difference in one's quality of life. As much as we might dread starting, exercise is one of those things we never regret having made time for when it is over. Teaching students to develop self-awareness about how they feel — not just physically, but emotionally and spiritually — when they choose to exercise and when they choose not to might be the most basic and life-giving thing a physical education class can give to every student.

I was never a good enough athlete to make a school team after elementary school, where everyone who tried out made it. But I was active in noon-hour intramural sports and, together with a group of friends, began playing slo-pitch softball on weekends through the spring and summer near the end of high school and through university. While I was never a star, I developed enough skill to play recreational league volleyball, floor hockey, football, and slo-pitch at various times throughout my years of postsecondary study. It is hard to calculate just how valuable this was to my life during that time. It meant meeting new friends and spending quality time with old ones; it meant staying active and getting regular exercise; it meant that, at a time when academic pressures threatened to take over my life, I had more balance; and it meant, perhaps more than all of these, a chance to relax, enjoy life, and have fun.

Indeed, this may be the most significant contribution of sport to human life in general, and a key reason sport is a universal in human culture. It is, in the end, an expression of the basic human longing for joy. There are moments in sport, competitive or recreational, where we lose track of time, where we are totally focused on what we are doing, where nothing matters but the present, where, at the same time, the pressures of life evaporate and boredom is not even conceivable. These moments are, in fact, glimpses of eternity.

SPORTS AS LENS ON REALITY

One interesting aspect of sports, from a Catholic point of view, is the way it witnesses to the objective character of reality. In a culture that is sometimes suspicious of claims about objective truth, sport has something essential to teach us. Consider how even the most ideologically committed relativist wants instant replay to overturn the call when their team has been the victim of an official's error. The puck either crossed the goal line or it didn't. The shot was released before the buzzer or it wasn't. The runner beat the throw by half a step or he didn't. In sports, reality is what it is. Relativism would make sports impossible.

Our culture is also often suspicious of rules. One reason for this is that we place such a high value on freedom. A Catholic will happily agree that, properly understood, freedom is a very high good indeed. But we also recognize that bad rules, not rules in general, impede freedom. Good rules, in fact, enable freedom to flourish. In the Book of Exodus, God gives the Israelites the law just as they have escaped slavery in Egypt. Freed from external oppression, from bad law, God gives them good law to keep them free. For the Jewish people, the law of God is not some externally imposed limit on human freedom, but the scaffolding on which interior freedom is built.

Freedom needs structure to thrive. Sports teach us this truth. The kind of creativity that we might see in a hockey shootout or an epic battle between pitcher and hitter are built on clear rules — the shooter must maintain forward motion, the pitcher must come set before moving into his delivery. Take away the structure provided by the rules, and the creativity has nothing to work with.

Our culture rightly values freedom and creativity, but it sometimes undercuts the very rules and structures needed to encourage genuine freedom and creativity. Young people, in particular, are looking for structure, not to oppress them, but to give them something to build on. Indeed, one reason for the growth in fundamentalism and extremism on both sides of our political spectrum is that people are searching for structure, for substantive claims about the nature of reality and the purpose of life. It is right to not want to burden young people with too many rules and expectations. But we must also avoid burdening them with a complete lack of rules and expectations. Sport is one place where our culture still recognizes that respect for the rules contributes to excellence. Indeed, if their expectations and rules are clear and consistent, our most beloved coaches and teachers are often those who demand the most of us.

Freedom and creativity are very valuable, but they are not ends in themselves. They enable us to do good and beautiful things and, through this, to encounter God. If we do not know what our freedom and creativity are for, not only are we more likely to misuse them, they may in fact slowly fade away. Like so many things, including sports, freedom and creativity need to be *practiced*. The saints are profoundly creative because they know what their freedom and creativity are for, and they practice using them well. They do not experience God's law as a limit on their freedom, but as a solid grounding for learning how to love well.

And nothing is more creative and free than love.

TRANSCENDENCE

Finally, like so many peak experiences in human life, sport points beyond itself. It is a strange thing that, in this life, we are never fully satisfied. We might work all season to win the championship. And if and when we do, we are startled to find that the satisfaction of that achievement, while real, is surprisingly fleeting. Or we might work for years, through high school and college, to make the big leagues. And if and when we do, we realize very quickly how the thing we dreamed of and worked towards for years does not fully satisfy. One athletic goal leads to another until, in very rare cases, one reaches the top — at which point it becomes clear, if it wasn't already, that life is about more than sports.

At a parish Lenten retreat I was giving, a young man approached me to ask a question that was troubling him greatly. He was a very skilled high school soccer player — one of the best in the province. His dream was to play professionally, and he wanted to know if that was God's plan for his life. The way he phrased the question made it clear to me that a negative answer would crush him. This put me in an awkward position. I knew full well that very few elite high school athletes ever make the big leagues and that, however good this young man was, his odds were very slim. I certainly couldn't tell him what (he thought) he wanted to hear. Instead, I told him that God had a plan for his life and desired something great for him. There was a chance, however slight, that that might involve playing professional soccer. But if it did not, that was because God had something even better in store.

This young man's desire to be a professional athlete was a desire for greatness, for a life that mattered. God put that desire into this young man, and he has given that same desire to every young person. Desire that seems unrealistic should be neither indulged ("Of course, you'll make the big leagues. You can do anything you put your mind to!") nor stifled ("You know, almost no one makes the big leagues. You should be more practical."); it should be channeled. All of our desires are, in the end, desire for God. Nothing in this world finally satisfies us because our desire is infinite. To pursue pleasure, glory, or power for their own sake is to pursue self-destruction, as many have learned. A Catholic education should encourage the kind of self-reflection that helps students see that sports are a window onto the infinity of human desire, a desire no worldly good or achievement can satisfy.

A CAUTION

It is good that young people desire strongly. But anything that can be mistaken for our *deepest desire* requires some caution. Recall that Thomas Aquinas encouraged sport and play in order to develop the virtue of moderation. But is it not often the case that sports themselves become the thing that needs moderating in our lives?

It is not for nothing that some people joke about sports being their religion. Interestingly, this might be truer of many fans than of the athletes themselves. But, whether for athletes or fans, it is possible for sports to be the place we seek most of our meaning, the place we spend most of our time, the thing that gets most of our energy, the thing for which all other things get sacrificed. In short, it is very easy for a person to have an unhealthy — even idolatrous — relationship with sports.

This can take a variety of forms. It might mean that a family stops going to Mass because the kids' sports have taken over their weekends. It might mean that a dad spends more time with ESPN than with his children. It might mean that a high school athlete drives herself into the ground chasing an elusive athletic scholarship, leading to a legacy of physical and emotional burnout. It might mean that a young person fails to develop other interests, like music or literature or philosophy or science, to say nothing of the practice of her faith, and loses out on the richness of life.

Like so many things that are good in themselves, sports can be all-consuming. Especially at a Catholic school, we should be careful that our elite athletes are learning to achieve balance and moderation in life, not letting their obligations to sports and team cancel out their obligations to academics, family, community, and God. No one is in a position to teach this like the coaches themselves. But the coaches will have no credibility to teach this if they do not first model it.

Finally, what is true of other potential stand-ins for God is true of sports as well. Sports can be a very satisfying part of a good life. But they cannot provide our deepest purpose or highest joy. If we ask them to, they will end up losing any ability to contribute to our purpose and joy at all. The sacrifices demanded by any false god are life-draining, not life-giving. How many young people have abandoned sports altogether because the pressure that came from parents and others took the joy entirely out of the game? Sports cannot bear that weight.

Sports and physical education are an essential part of any education. Their capacity for building virtue and community and the joy, even the glimpses of transcendence, they can provide demand the attention of anyone thinking about how to make an education truly Catholic. If students learn in a Catholic school how to integrate sport and fitness into a balanced life, giving them not too much and not too little importance, both their bodies and their souls will benefit.

Assignment Idea: Exercise Journal

A key goal of any physical education curriculum is to develop healthy long-term exercise habits. But teaching that exercising is good and not exercising is bad is only the beginning of such a process. Any real change of habits needs to engage with a person's need and capacity for making meaning. Journaling about our experiences is an excellent way to achieve this.

Have students make an exercise plan for some specific length of time — for example, a week, a month — and try to stick to it. But the heart of the assignment is not making the plan or even doing the exercise, but journaling about the experience of trying to make and stick to an exercise plan. What are the feelings that emerge through this process and what do they mean? What do my reactions say about what I really think or believe? How do I feel when I meet my goals and when I struggle to meet them?

Moreover, journaling is not only a place to think about our habits; it is itself a habit that can be life-changing. While reactive journaling — reflecting on how we feel after the fact — is powerful, so is proactive journaling, where we envision our day and make plans for how to deal with problems we know we can expect to encounter. These two elements can create a healthy and powerful feedback loop in the formation of good habits.

If spirituality is, as we explored in chapter 10, the beliefs and practices we employ to make sense of our world and to try to live well in it, beliefs and practices about exercise are a part of our spirituality. This could be done cross-curricularly with health class, making exercise one element of a larger self-examination about beliefs and habits.

KEY TAKEAWAYS

Catholic emphasis on the goodness of the body is rooted in our doctrine of creation and, especially, our belief in the resurrection of the body.

Given the unity of body and soul, the physical is never just the physical. Health and fitness, including sports, therefore have an important role to play in the Christian life.

Sports are a great context for the development of virtue — and not only for those playing at a high level. A Catholic education understands the role and value of sports for everyone.

In a culture that is often suspicious of rules, sports highlight the value of good rules and the right relationship between rules and freedom.

Sports can give us a glimpse of transcendence but, like any earthly good, sports need to be part of a balanced life. Our relationship with sport can become idolatrous.

Chapter 12
Art

Several of the themes explored in the chapter on literature (chapter 5) are of obvious relevance to art. Literature is, after all, an art form. And while we had occasion in that chapter to pay particular attention to the power of words, many of the features of a Catholic worldview that we explored have a parallel impact in the arts more generally. Indeed, the question, "Why does the Church produce so much great literature?" that we explored in that chapter needs to be expanded to, "Why does the Church produce so much great art?" The Church has produced not only writers, but painters, sculptors, architects, composers, and filmmakers, to name just a few. The Catholic imagination is fertile soil for all kinds of artistic engagement. Indeed, a Catholic imagination is not only fruitful for the production of art, but for its appreciation and enjoyment. Most of our students will not grow up to be professional artists, but all of them will have richer lives if they can engage with the truth, goodness, and beauty of reality through the medium of the arts.

OBJECTIVE TRUTH

Art flourishes when it strives to represent and respond to reality. This does not mean that the only good painting is one that is photorealistic. Or that literature can never explore reality through genres like fantasy or science fiction. Rather, it means that any approach the artist employs, however abstract or fantastical, should help us to see reality more clearly. Think of a cartoonist or a stand-up comic. Their exaggerations and absurdities, used well, do not obscure the real, but illuminate it. Many of Charles Dickens's greatest characters, for example, are cartoonish embodiments of genuine human qualities. The genius of Dickens is to teach us true things about ourselves precisely through such exaggerated characters. The same can be true of the visual arts. I remember being stunned the first time I saw a Caravaggio. I felt as though, here, the art of painting had been perfected because it seemed so real. But a Caravaggio is not how the world typically looks. Rather, through his signature dramatic use of light and shade, Caravaggio makes his paintings seem almost more real than reality itself! And Jesus' parables do not need to be literally true in order for them to convey deep truths about humanity and our situation before God. The numbers given in the parable of the unforgiving servant (Mt 18:23–35) are clearly unrealistic. But it is just those unrealistic numbers that express the real generosity of God.

To say that good art strives to represent the real, then, is not a straitjacket on the artist, limiting their creativity and imagination. It is a goal that inspires creativity. If there is a world beyond me and meaning inherent in that world beyond what I myself make of it, I am challenged to know, engage with, and represent that world as it is. Such a challenge leads to insight and beauty and even to communion with others who share that reality. But if not, if *I* am the measure of all things, then there is nothing outside of me by which my art may be evaluated. Art then becomes self-referential by definition, and art appreciation starts to feel like a guessing game.

We have all been trapped in banal and inaccessible conversations with people who, however knowledgeable and intelligent they may be, are dreadful bores because they talk only of themselves. Art is like a conversation; nothing kills it like self-referentiality. It is not belief in the real beyond oneself that is limiting, but the belief that I determine for myself what is true and real. To affirm *that* is to go from inhabiting a vast and mysterious and glorious creation, one that I share with the rest of humanity and one in which art can flourish, to a cramped, lonely world of one, where art becomes more and more arbitrary and less and less intelligible to any hoped-for audience.

It is often imagined that freedom and creativity thrive when restraints are removed. And it is certainly true that *some* restraints, like fear of failure, for instance, can impede creativity. But it is also true that other kinds of restraints foster creativity. The rules of a sport, or musical scales, or even moral prohibitions all provide the scaffolding needed for athletic, musical, or ethical virtuosity. In the same way, respecting the restraints of reality empowers and frees the artist. It was Michelangelo's deep knowledge of and respect for perspective that allowed him to create, in both *David* and in the *Pietà*, sculptures that look right even while their proportions are, compared to actual human bodies, outlandish.

GOD AS ARTIST

Of the thousands of images I have seen from a telescope,
I've never seen anything ugly in space.

BROTHER GUY CONSOLMAGNO,
DIRECTOR, VATICAN OBSERVATORY

Because of the Christian doctrine of creation, one of the most important and fruitful metaphors we have for thinking about God is God as artist. The Bible has regular recourse to the notion of God as builder or craftsman, laying foundations under the earth or working clay on a potter's wheel. Even Mary Magdalene's mistaking the risen Jesus for the gardener is a reference to God as artist: Jesus is not just any gardener; he is the very gardener of Eden. In the profound creation story Tolkien wrote for Middle Earth, the Ainulindalë, God is a composer and choir director, and the angelic beings are singers. The idea of history as a drama — "all the world's a stage" — is so common that we almost need to be reminded that it is a metaphor. And the notion that a sunset is God painting is almost a truism. From the clichéd to the sublime, the metaphor of God as artist is everywhere.

In fact, it is so common we might think that it is obvious and even unremarkable. But this is only because we have lost touch with just how revolutionary the biblical notion of God really is. For much of human history, God did not paint sunsets or mountainscapes; rather, gods themselves were perceived in these images of natural beauty and power. The human proclivity is to worship creation in place of the Creator. And this is just as true when we worship the economy or the nation state or ourselves as it was when our ancestors worshipped mountains and rivers.

Like the idea of creating by speech rather than by violence that we saw in chapter 5, the image of God as artist is a way of expressing the biblical God's transcendent relationship to creation. Yes, creation is beautiful and powerful, but this beauty and power points beyond itself to the beauty and power of the Creator. Have you ever noticed that a magnificent sunset or a stunning piece of music does not so much satisfy our deepest longings as intensify them? Truly beautiful art, like nature that is the "art" of God, points beyond itself. It awakens and focuses desire that can only be satisfied by Beauty itself. This is one reason art has historically been such an important part of the Church's efforts of evangelization. In a Catholic art class, the recognition of the sacramental relationship between created and uncreated beauty will form both Catholic artists and Catholics who truly appreciate art.

ART AS SUBCREATION

We make in our measure and in our derivative mode, because we are made: and not only made, but made in the image and likeness of a Maker.

J. R. R. TOLKIEN

It is important to remind ourselves, of course, that metaphors for speaking about God are just that. Catholic theology insists that it is possible to speak of God intelligibly, but it also insists that we recognize that our language will always come up short. And so, when we use metaphors to speak of God, it is as instructive to attend to where those metaphors break down as to where they work.

To speak of God as an artist is to employ something from human experience in order to try and say something both intelligible and true about God. But it is essential to recognize that this metaphor, like all metaphors, is imperfect. In the case of God as artist, the most significant gap between the metaphor and the reality it is trying to communicate is the fact that artists work with pre-existing, given, materials, and God creates *ex nihilo*, from nothing.

This is the key distinction between what Tolkien calls "subcreation" and creation proper. The act of creation itself is only possible for a transcendent God; any acts of subcreation presume and build upon that initial creative act. This is why good art begins with the virtue of humility. Artists must be humble before reality — *before creation* — as they find it. Any true artist is first an honest and perceptive observer. This does not mean that it is the job of the artist merely to replicate what he sees. An essential task of the artist is to show us how things *might be*. But that task is impossible for the person who does not see and understand how things *are*. And one does not need to be a professional artist for this to be true. Both the amateur artist and the person who lives a fuller life through appreciating art made by others derive great benefit from humility before reality, including the reality that is art itself.

An artist must also be humble before the tradition of art. In every field of human endeavor, from science and sport to prayer and parenting, those who achieve greatness invariably learn from those who have gone before. This does not mean innovation is bad. It means that good innovation comes from deep familiarity with tradition. And so, the study of art history and the cultivation of art appreciation are, in addition to helping everyone understand and enjoy art, essential to the development of an artistic vocation. Even something as seemingly menial as copying great works of art is, in fact, one of the best ways of learning the craft. This runs counter to our contemporary image of authentic artists as rebels and iconoclasts. But even iconoclasm is a tradition! There is nothing wrong with challenging a dominant narrative. Indeed, such prophetic work can be one of the most noble tasks of the artist. But this does not imply that the artist is somehow free from tradition. The Sermon on the Mount could only have been preached by someone who knew both *the law and the prophets* — i.e., the tradition, including the critical voices within it — from his youth.

Third, an artist must be humble before the demands of his chosen craft. God creates out of nothing. Human artists work with what is already given. Oil and canvas, chisel and stone, light and shadow, are intransigent elements of creation. They will only submit themselves to the person who first submits to the demands of their nature. Even words and their meanings can feel as stubborn as wood or stone, as any writer knows. An artist in a funk feels his materials resisting him. At their creative best, though, artists do not experience themselves as dominating reality but as cooperating with it. Sometimes — as when a sculptor imagines liberating an almost pre-existing statue from a block of marble, or when a poet feels like a conduit for words that were just waiting to be written — artists even describe the materials as themselves directing the process. What such experiences indicate is a harmony with reality that is the fruitful soil of so much great art.

ART AND LONGING

The human mind, endowed with the powers of generalization and abstraction, sees not only green grass, discriminating it from other things (and finding it fair to look upon), but sees that it is green as well as being grass. But how powerful, how stimulating to the very faculty that produced it, was the invention of the adjective: no spell or incantation in Faerie is more potent.

J. R. R. Tolkien

At the root of the human capacity for art is the ability to abstract from reality as it is and imagine it differently. It is only creatures that can distinguish green from green grass that can conceive both unicorns and utopias — or dragons and dystopias! As much as art must be rooted in honest observation of reality, it is not content with simply portraying reality as it is. Our greatest artists are very often those among us who are particularly sensitive to the universal human desire for something more. To put this in theological terms, art is eschatological.

Eschatology is often described as the study of the four last things: death, judgment, heaven, and hell. And this is true as far as it goes. But, at a deeper level, eschatology is about God's transformation of creation that, while it will only be complete on the last day, began already with the Resurrection. An eschatological imagination perceives the working of the Holy Spirit in history and in individual human lives, knowing that hope is more real than any darkness. This also is humility before reality. From a Catholic point of view, the deepest reality of the world is not its brokenness, as real as that is, but its blessedness. It is true that I am a sinner; it is more true — or, at least, more importantly true — that I am a beloved child of God. Theologians often speak of eschatology in terms of the "already" and the "not yet" to emphasize that, while God's work in Christ is definitive, it awaits its final fulfillment. Christ has died; Christ is risen; Christ will come again.

Good art does not need to be Christian to point to this eschatological reality. In a Catholic art class, we should draw attention to the desire for something more that underlies so much great art. From The Rolling Stones' "I Can't Get No Satisfaction" to U2's "I Still Haven't Found What I'm Looking For" and beyond, rock music is often an exploration of unfulfilled desire. The infamous "rock and roll lifestyle" is a study in looking for love — and transcendence — in all the wrong places. But the longing at the heart of rock music is a genuine expression of the longing for God in every human heart.

"Paradise City," by Guns' n' Roses, is a glorious (I use the term deliberately) example of art that looks reality in the face and cries out for something more. It opens with soaring, anthemic guitars soon overlaid with the iconic chorus in evocative, layered vocals (note the green grass!). The energy builds until, at a key point, someone blows a harsh whistle, the guitar shifts to a sequence of gritty power chords, and the first verse begins to describe life on the street in a raspy scream. The basic dynamic of the song is the alternation of the angry, desperate verses and the melodic, wistful chorus, a back and forth between reality as it is and reality as it might be. The tension rises until, at the end of the last chorus, the final word, "home," is repeated and held longer and higher than seems possible before the band goes into a double-time outro that embodies nothing so much as a frantic and harried search while the singer begs and begs for some assurance that he will finally be taken home.

"Paradise City" is an eschatological masterpiece. Even as the singer is left in a state of desperate pursuit without resolution, the song evokes in the listener the desire for rest, for acceptance, for beauty, for home, for God. As John Paul II wrote in his *Letter to Artists*, "Even when they explore the darkest depths of the soul or the most unsettling aspects of evil, artists give voice in a way to the universal desire for redemption." The questions and desires at the heart of human experience have always inspired artists. And so, art is always a window to the human soul and an approach to the mystery that is God, even when the artist does not know it. A Catholic art class, then, is not satisfied with the teaching of technique, but always recognizes art as part of humanity's search for meaning, and ultimately, for God. Art class is a privileged place to wrestle with life's big questions.

PRAYER OR PROPAGANDA?

Indeed, art can be a form of prayer, even for the unbeliever. Everyone who seeks truth, seeks God. As art is so often a pursuit of truth, it is the pursuit of God and, therefore, prayer. For the Christian artist — and the art student in your class — this can be made quite explicit. The artist may well put himself into God's hands as he prepares a given work. He may consciously seek the inspiration of the Holy Spirit. He may convey explicitly religious truth. In the creation of sacred art, these are not options but basic requirements. But we can also recognize that approaches to these realities often happen unconsciously, as an artist honestly seeks the truth about himself or the world and attempts to portray that truth in his art.

Whether this is done consciously and intentionally or not, the common denominator is the desire to know and reveal the true. If, on the other hand, truth is not the goal, art becomes impossible. I don't mean that one cannot paint, or sculpt, or make films without seeking truth. Rather, I mean that any work produced in this way will not be art in the proper sense. As we have seen, much contemporary thought imagines either that truth does not exist in any meaningful way, or at least that we do not have access to it. If this is the case, if there is nothing beyond ourselves by which we might be measured, then all we are left with, as Nietzsche clearly saw, is the pursuit of power. Like the rest of a Catholic education, art class must be part of our pursuit of truth. In it we learn both to communicate and to perceive truth.

Art that honestly seeks truth will be powerful to the degree that it succeeds in rendering that truth. But art that seeks power for its own sake ceases to be art and becomes mere propaganda. It may retain influence in this form, but that influence will be an influence of coercion and manipulation that sows the seeds of its own rejection as it builds distrust and resentment in its audience. Indeed, to the degree that any society has abandoned the pursuit of the truth in favor of the pursuit of power, it has lost its capacity for art.

The temptation to reduce art to propaganda is very great. This is especially the case as the public negotiation of power and its use — what we call "politics" — has become for many, including not a few Christians, the most important reality. Politics is always tempted to totalizing claims, and it is an essential task of religion to relativize such claims. As important as the ordering of our communities through the political process is, Christians must always seek God's kingdom before the goals of any earthly kingdom. It is when Christians themselves start to treat politics as ultimate that "Christian art" becomes insufferable. Many have lamented the lack of artistic value, for instance, in "Christian" films that seem to be morals in search of a story. And many have argued that certain excellent works of art that explore truth in beautiful and compelling ways are, in a way, more Christian than many works produced and marketed as "Christian," no matter the religious commitments of the artist.

Not that Christians are the only ones reducing art to propaganda. Far from it! Indeed, teachers might be more likely to encounter this temptation in all kinds of "socially conscious" art projects than in "moralistic" ones. I only note this phenomenon so that aspiring Christian artists might be forewarned and so that Christian audiences might better understand why so much "Christian art" feels so inadequate. It is easy to produce propaganda instead of art when we live in a world awash in propaganda and we have not developed the tools we need to sift the wheat from the chaff. But, as Tolkien made clear in *The Lord of the Rings*, to resort to using the enemy's weapons is to guarantee our own defeat; even when we win, we lose.

ART AND EVANGELIZATION

The only really effective apologia for Christianity comes down to two arguments, namely, the saints the Church has produced and the art which has grown in her womb.

JOSEPH RATZINGER

In this book, and in many other contexts, you may have noticed the terms *truth, goodness,* and *beauty* appearing together. These are the so-called transcendentals, and they are attributes of all created beings. They transcend any particulars of time, space, and culture, and point to the origin and unity of all things in God. This is one reason Catholics can be so confident both that truth (and goodness and beauty) is available in human culture more generally, even before an encounter with Divine Revelation, and that the truth (and goodness and beauty) of the Gospel is accessible to all people regardless of the particulars of their historical and cultural setting. Truth, goodness, and beauty are things that all people value and can perceive in the world around them. They are, therefore, avenues of encounter with created reality, with one another, and with God.

Catholic thought has been fascinated with the relationship between these three transcendentals. Because of their basic underlying unity in God, if something is true, and to the degree that it is true, it is also good and beautiful. And this correlation works in every direction. To the degree something is good, it is true and beautiful. And to the degree something is beautiful, it is also true and good. Different aspects of human life and culture may seem to lead more with one or the other of the three, but its two companions are always present. A math proof might seem to have more to do with truth, but it is also good and beautiful. An act of generosity is obviously good, but it is also true and beautiful. A painting may arrest our attention with its beauty, but contemplation of it will reveal its truth and goodness as well. These relationships help us understand the surprising line from Cardinal Ratzinger. The saints are good, and art is beautiful. These two point, then, to the truth of the Catholic Faith.

If this is the case, it is not hard to see that art can make a profound contribution to the work of evangelization. In pursuing and revealing the beautiful, art simultaneously pursues and reveals the good and the true. This is one reason that Pope John Paul II, in his *Letter to Artists*, can call art "a kind of bridge to religious experience." He continues, "In so far as it seeks the beautiful, fruit of an imagination which rises above the everyday, art is by its nature a kind of appeal to the mystery." Much is made about the importance of the Catholic science teacher in the Church's work of evangelization, and rightly so. But the role of the art teacher is indispensable. For the art teacher works in the field where humans have always, almost instinctively, explored their deepest questions.

In our increasingly post-Christian culture, appeals to truth are often met with suspicion. And while much of what we understand as goodness is obvious and commonly agreed upon, there are more and more areas of our common life where what actually constitutes the good is openly contested. There are many people who find this state of affairs unsatisfying and even exhausting. For some of these folks, appeals to truth and goodness can be effective ways of presenting the Gospel. But for many contemporary people, such appeals are easily dismissed. In such a context, beauty, and therefore art, has a profound role to play in our presentation of the Gospel.

Have you ever noticed that many conversion stories begin with someone feeling mysteriously called to simply enter a Catholic church and sit in silence? Beauty often touches people in a way that logical argument cannot. Beautiful churches should not be underestimated as tools for evangelization. And art in general is equipped to deal with the profound questions we humans ask ourselves in ways that go beyond what reason alone can offer. While its primary goal may be to show us the beautiful, when it does that task well, art also helps us to see goodness and truth.

Take the problem of suffering, for instance. Many people today recognize that the presence of suffering in the world is one of the best arguments against the existence of a good and loving God. And they are right! It is. Christians need to be able to respond to this concern. The logical argument that God permits suffering out of respect for human freedom is not wrong, but it can feel inadequate in the face of great pain. Art can show us how even suffering can be part of something beautiful. It is a remarkable feature of human life that each of us has elements of suffering in our past that we would not trade. While we would never have chosen the suffering at the time, we now appreciate that our lives, our relationships, and our character have been shaped by the experience of suffering in ways that we deeply value.

Artists communicate this reality in profound and compelling ways, often because they have reflected deeply on their own suffering. There is a long tradition of great art born of suffering. And this gives such art depth and authenticity when it confronts the problem of suffering. While it should never be sought for its own sake, suffering can nevertheless become part of something beautiful. Have you ever seen a photograph of the wrinkle-creased face of an elderly person whose life has obviously seen its share of suffering that unaccountably strikes you as beautiful? Or take a moment to think of your own favorite novel or movie. Try to imagine how that story would be impacted if all the suffering were eliminated. Would it be more beautiful without those elements of suffering? Now, think of your own life and ask the same question.

This is not to say that suffering is a positive good. Indeed, that is one of the dangers of logical argument that art helps us to avoid! Certain logical responses to the problem of suffering can almost make it sound like suffering should be sought out, or at least that we need not work to eliminate it. Art is much better equipped to strike the balance that says both that we must work to combat suffering whenever possible, and that suffering can be part of something beautiful.

Consider: God's own response to suffering was not a logical argument, but a drama, his own entry into our broken human history. From the drama that was the life, death, and resurrection of Jesus we learn both that God desires to heal the suffering world — indeed, that he has so identified himself with the most despised and downtrodden that we will be judged by our treatment of them — and that God can redeem even the most senseless suffering and evil, incorporating everything into his loving plan for creation. Even as it affirms that God can use suffering for his own higher purposes, the Gospel does not let us off the hook for alleviating the sufferings of our world. That is great art.

LIFE AS A WORK OF ART

All men and women are entrusted with the task of crafting their own life: in a certain sense, they are to make of it a work of art, a masterpiece.

POPE ST. JOHN PAUL II

The Book of Genesis tells us that humanity was put in the Garden of Eden in order to till and keep it. This primordial image of subcreation — working with materials already given by God — is symbolic of humanity's task of stewardship over all creation. Built into creation from the start are potentialities that will only be realized by humans pursuing our call to create within creation. This is one reason why the Bible begins with a garden and ends, in the Book of Revelation, with a city — the new Jerusalem. A garden is a symbol of nature. A city is a symbol of human culture. But, unlike the tower of Babel, a symbol of a corrupt culture that tried to reach God on its own terms, the new Jerusalem is a symbol of redeemed culture. Instead of ascending from the earth, like the tower of Babel, we see it descending from the heavens. Even the greatest achievements of humanity are, properly understood, gifts from God.

An artist, then, is a steward of creation. By using his God-given talent to form and shape the God-given material order, the artist develops the potential of creation. This is both a service to our neighbors and a contribution to the patrimony of all humanity. The Bible is not specific on this point, but we probably do not go too far astray to imagine the new Jerusalem crowded with splendid museums and libraries and theaters showcasing the glories of human artistic achievement. But let us imagine them not simply as they are in history, but as somehow elevated by grace. In a wonderful short story, "Leaf by Niggle," Tolkien fancies that imperfect and inadequate works of art will await their creators in the afterlife in their completeness. Here again, inasmuch as no work ever quite captures the ideal in the mind of the artist, we see the eschatological nature of art. The painful gap between conception and execution that every artist experiences is a longing for a perfection that is not available in this life.

In this, art and artists tell us something about humanity more generally. We are all of us — mathematicians, groundskeepers, engineers, doctors, parents, teachers — stewards of creation in some way or other. We all have care of some element of creation whose potential we are called to nurture and develop. But, regardless of our particular vocation in this life, we are also stewards of the creature that is ourselves. And what most determines how we are able to shape the world is the degree to which we can ourselves be shaped. As John Paul II wrote in his *Letter to Artists*, "Through his 'artistic creativity' man appears more than ever 'in the image of God', and he accomplishes this task above all in shaping the wondrous 'material' of his own humanity and then exercising creative dominion over the universe which surrounds him."

The task of the artist is to translate the spiritual into the material, to present to humanity the true and the good in the form of the beautiful. But this is only a specific and paradigmatic instance of the basic human situation. All human lives are the translations of the immaterial — values, ideas, hopes, prejudices, fears — into the realm of the material. Every story we tell ourselves, every choice we make, literally *embodies* the spiritual. In this we again image our Creator.

If God can be fruitfully thought of as an artist, then the Incarnation is God's masterpiece. In the Incarnation, God, who is invisible spirit, becomes visible for us; God, who is ineffable, is spoken to us as a Word. Marshall McLuhan was a faithful Catholic, and he understood communications media — a form of art — from a Catholic point of view. His famous aphorism, "the medium is the message," is, before it is anything else, a Christological statement. In the person and life of Jesus, God's medium is God's message and vice versa. The same is true of each one of us. The medium that is our lives is the message we share with the world.

Assignment Idea: Exploring Catholic Artists

Catholicism has produced great artists across the whole range of human artistic endeavor. In whatever medium you are exploring, have students choose a Catholic artist to study. Students can write a report exploring the artist's context, achievements, technique, and, essentially, ideas about faith and art. Such a report can be written, presented, or both. This report is preliminary to the more substantial element of this assignment: to create a piece of art in the spirit of the artist under study.

Depending on the student and the objectives being pursued, this piece could be a replication of one of the artist's pieces (do not underestimate the learning that can be achieved through an attempt at replication!) or an original piece in the style of that artist. While sacred art is certainly important in our Catholic artistic heritage, it is also important that we do not give students the impression that the only art which is influenced by faith is specifically sacred art. Accordingly, students can certainly choose an artist whose oeuvre extends beyond sacred art.

Note: This basic idea could also be applied to a music class and composition.

KEY TAKEAWAYS

Good art is not arbitrary, but ordered toward representing truth and beauty. This does not impede, but rather frees the artist. In a Catholic art class, students should learn that art is responsible to reality.

Imagining God as an artist is a key metaphor in the Christian tradition. Christian artists can fruitfully understand their own vocation to art as "subcreators" who humbly work with what is already given by God in creation.

Humans use art to express their desire for something more. In a Catholic art class, this dynamic should be explored in terms of our universal desire for God.

Art that pursues truth is a form of prayer (for the artist and, potentially, the audience). Art that pursues power is reduced to propaganda.

Art has an essential role in evangelization and is a great place to explore deep human questions, like the problem of suffering.

Each of us is called to make our lives a work of art, a translation of our deepest values into the material realm of time and space in which we live.

Conclusion
Now, It's Your Turn

"You can't start a fire without a spark."

BRUCE SPRINGSTEEN, "DANCING IN THE DARK"

In the original conception of this book, what became Part II was imagined as one concluding chapter with some brief comments and maybe an example or two for each subject area. Then the Catholic Teachers' Guild of Regina invited me to give a lecture series on curriculum permeation (what we call Catholic Academic Integration in this part of the world). Like many Catholic teachers, they were being asked to do something in their classrooms that most of them had not received any training for in their undergraduate study or in subsequent professional development. They knew that they were supposed to infuse each class with a Catholic worldview, but they didn't always know how. Could I help them?

As I prepared each session's material, I was amazed at how much there was to talk about as we approached each subject with our Catholic lenses on. The difficulty was not filling an hour, but stopping after only an hour. It became clear to me and to the teachers of the guild that we were only scratching the surface and that, once we really wrapped our heads around how Catholicism informed our teaching of each subject area, our classrooms would be transformed.

And so, chapter 5 became Part II, and eight subject areas got a more thorough treatment than I had originally imagined was possible. But the feeling that I am only scratching the surface remains. For one thing, there are many more subject areas taught in our schools than the eight treated here. And Catholic business and music and computer and psychology teachers, to name just a few more, all need to think about their subjects from a Catholic point of view just as much as the history and science teachers. But I needed to draw a line somewhere (though I did manage to sneak at least a little music into the Math and Art chapters). I sincerely hope that others, with more expertise than me in these areas and others, will be inspired to think and write about how their Catholic faith shapes their teaching and their classrooms. I'd love to hear from you if you do!

In addition to leaving out whole subject areas, I had to be selective about what to include in the chapters I did write. It would have been a very legitimate choice, for instance, to devote the Civics and Social Studies chapter largely to a study of Catholic Social Teaching. I did not go this route for the simple reason that there are already great resources on Catholic Social Teaching available. And the History chapter could have been dedicated to debunking anti-Catholic narratives common in our culture (and sometimes even in our curricula) one by one. Again, this is valuable and necessary work. But others have already done it well. Given the tension between the Church and the broader culture on the question, the Health chapter could have justifiably focused a lot more on sex and relationships. In this case, I was happy to be able to recommend one of my own books (written with my friend Leah Perrault). The temptation to write whole other books — for example, on politics and voting, or on creation and evolution — crept up regularly as I worked on this book. It was nice to have at least one of them already written.

Finally, this book could not do all the work of turning the ideas in each chapter into curricula, unit plans, and lesson plans. I offered a few ideas and examples to kindle the imagination, but teachers, not theologians, are the real professionals here. Moreover, much of that boots-on-the-ground kind of work needs to be done at the local level, in dialogue with the curricula to which we are each responsible in our own contexts. It is my hope that many of the folks doing this work will find a community in the Making Every Class Catholic Facebook group, where we can share resources and ideas.

My goal in this book was to introduce into the reader's imagination the possibility of viewing each area of study from a Catholic point of view, not to say everything there is to say about every subject. I wanted to make a certain kind of thought more thinkable. If I have been successful, you should now be able to approach all kinds of material that I did not specifically cover with your Catholic lenses on and see things you would not have seen before. I pray that God may bless your efforts as you take what you have learned and work to make every class Catholic.

Acknowledgments

It is a paradox that, while writing is solitary work, a book like this would not exist without the support of a community. I want to thank Father John Meehan, SJ, for inviting me to teach a Philosophy of Catholic Education course at Campion College, where I first began thinking about the questions that inspired this book. And my students from that first class, for thinking through these issues with me and for their commitment to Catholic education. Thank you to Miles Myers and Delmer Wagner, my first mentors in the idea of curriculum permeation here in Saskatchewan, and to the Catholic Teachers' Guild of Regina for inviting me to consider these questions with them in depth.

Thank you to Kevin Campbell, Deacon Joe Lang, Tannis Scott, LeeAnn Arsenault, Mark Siolek, Paul d'Hondt, Peter Bagnall, and Karen Tigani for sharing with me the privilege of working with Catholic teachers across Canada. Thank you to Deacon Eric Gurash, my friend and cohost on the *Thinking Faith!* Podcast, where several episodes have been dedicated to the ideas in this book, and to various guests over the years — including but not limited to Honni Lizee, Thomas Quackenbush, Andrew Seeley, Jessica Hooten Wilson, André Polaniecki, and Dan Guernsey — who have helped me consider what Catholicism means for different subject areas. I almost never listen to my own podcast, but I did go back and listen to you as I drafted these chapters.

Thank you to Ryan LeBlanc, Catholic teacher extraordinaire, for early conversations as this book took shape. To the crew at the McGrath Center for Church Life at the University of Notre Dame and *Church Life Journal* — Artur Rosman, Christopher Baglow, John Cavadini, Tim O'Malley, Jess Keating — for your support of my work in general and this project in particular, many thanks. Thanks to Mary Beth Giltner, my editor at OSV, who "got" this project immediately and supported me in a multitude of ways through a longer than hoped for drafting process. Thanks to Denise Donohue of the Cardinal Newman Society for her time and expertise offering feedback on Part I; and to Brett Fawcett, a fount of insight and knowledge, for reading and offering excellent feedback on each chapter, for joining us on *Thinking Faith!*, and for helping manage the Making Every Class Catholic Facebook group.

To the director of pastoral services here in the Archdiocese of Regina, Lisa Polk, and my archbishop, Donald Bolen, for your support of my writing in a world where the crisis *du jour* always threatens to become all-consuming and projects like books can be pushed back indefinitely. Your conviction that I have something to offer the larger Church is one of the reasons I love my job. Thanks to Michael O'Brien, for a generous and insightful conversation as I drafted the Art chapter, and to John O'Brien, SJ, for arranging said conversation.

Last, but not least, to Flannery, Toby, Oscar, Daisy, Dorothy, Beatrice, Sebastian, and Martha, my wife, sons, and daughters in whom I delight and with whom I am well-pleased: thank you.

Just typing your names brings me great joy. I love you all! Now that "the book" is done, let's play more games and go for more bike rides.

Works Cited

Part I: What Are People For?
Augustine of Hippo. *Confessions.*
Dickens, Charles. *Hard Times.* Wordsworth Classics, 1995.

Chapter 1: Joy, Virtue, and Holiness
Augustine of Hippo. *Confessions.*
Bloy, Léon. *The Woman Who Was Poor.* 1897.
Wallace, David Foster. "This is Water." 2005 Kenyon College Commencement address. May 21, 2005.

Chapter 2: Truth and Freedom
Davis, Pete. "A Counterculture of Commitment." 2018 Harvard Commencement Address. May 24, 2018.
McLuhan, Marshall. *Understanding Media: The Extensions of Man.* 1964.
Newman, John Henry. "Hope in God the Creator." *Meditations on Christian Doctrine.* March 7, 1848.
Orwell, George. *1984.* 1949.

Chapter 3: Faith and Reason
Anselm. *Proslogion.*
Augustine. *Tractates on the Gospel of John.*
John Paul II. *Fides et Ratio.* September 14, 1998.

Chapter 4: Catholicism Makes Everything Interesting
Benedict XVI. Address to the Bishops of the United States of America. May 5, 2012.
de Lubac, Henri. *Paradoxes of Faith.* 1948.
Percy, Walker. *Signposts in a Strange Land.* New York: Picador,

1991.

Postman, Neil. *The End of Education: Redefining the Value of School.* New York: Vintage Books, 1996.

Part II: Catholic Academic Integration

Baglow, Christopher. "Catholic Academic Integration: Science, Literature, History." *Church Life Journal.* March 8, 2022.

Congregation for Catholic Education. *The Catholic School on the Threshold of the Third Millennium.* December 28, 1997.

Paul VI, *Gaudium et Spes* (Pastoral Constitution on the Church in the Modern World). December 7, 1965.

Chapter 5: Literature and Language Arts

John Paul II. *Letter to Artists.* April 4, 1999.

Justin Martyr. *First Apology.*

Lewis, C.S. *The Weight of Glory.* 1949.

Nietzsche, Friedrich. *The Twilight of the Idols and The Anti-Christ, or How to Philosophize with a Hammer.*

O'Connor, Flannery. "Catholic Novelists and Their Readers" in *Mystery and Manners*, ed. Sally and Robert Fitzgerald. New York: Farrar, Straus & Giroux, 1969.

Chapter 6: History

Cavanaugh, William T. *The Myth of Religious Violence: Secular Ideology and the Roots of Modern Conflict.* Oxford University Press, 2009.

Sacks, Rabbi Jonathan. BBC RE:THINK Festival, debate with Richard Dawkins. September 12, 2012.

Visser, Margaret. *Beyond Fate.* 2002 Massey Lectures. Toronto: House of Anansi Press Inc, 2002.

Chapter 8: Science

Aquinas, Thomas. *Commentary on Aristotle's Physics.*

———. *Summa Contra Gentiles.*

———. *Summa Theologiae.*

Augustine. *On the Literal Meaning of Genesis.*

Baglow, Christopher. *Creation: A Catholic's Guide to God and the Universe.* Notre Dame, IN: Ave Maria Press, 2021.

Barr, Stephen M. *Science and Religion: The Myth of Conflict.* Great Britain: Catholic Truth Society, 2011.

Benedict XVI. Homily from the Mass for the Inauguration of the Pontificate. April 24, 2005.

———. *"In the Beginning...": A Catholic Understanding of the Story of Creation and the Fall,* trans. Boniface Ramsey, OP. Grand Rapids, MI: William B. Eerdmans Publishing Company, 1995.

———. *Spe Salvi.* November 30, 2007.

John Paul II. Letter to Fr. George Coyne, SJ, Director of the Vatican Observatory. June 1, 1988.

Kuebler, Daniel. "The Purposeful Universe — A Conversation with Dr. Dan Kuebler." Magis Center video.

Legge, OP, Dominic. "Intro to Primary and Secondary Causality." Video. Aquinas 101. The Thomistic Institute.

Medi, Enrico quoted in Benedict XVI. "General Audience." March 24, 2010.

Newman, John Henry. Letter to J. Walker of Scarborough on Darwin's Theory of Evolution. May 22, 1868.

Stark, Rodney. *Bearing False Witness: Debunking Centuries of Anti-Catholic History.* West Conshohocken, PA: Templeton Press, 2016.

Chapter 9: Civics and Social Studies

Francis, *Laudato Si'.* May 24, 2015.

King Jr., Martin Luther. "Letter from Birmingham Jail." April 16,

1963.

Paul VI. *Nostra Aetate* (Declaration on the Relation of the Church to Non-Christian Religions). October 28, 1965.

Pontifical Council for Justice and Peace, *Compendium of the Social Doctrine of the Church.* 2004.

Shea, Mark. *The Church's Best Kept Secret: A Primer on Catholic Social Teaching.* New York: New City Press, 2020.

United Nations. *Universal Declaration on Human Rights.* 1948.

Chapter 10: Health

Lehner, Ulrich. *God Is Not Nice: Rejecting Pop Culture Theology and Discovering the God Worth Living For.* Notre Dame, IN: Ave Maria Press, 2017.

Perrault, Leah and Brett Salkeld. *How Far Can We Go? A Catholic Guide to Sex and Dating.* Mahwah, NJ: Paulist Press, 2011.

Ratzinger, Joseph. *Called to Communion: Understanding the Church Today*, trans. Adrian Walker. San Francisco: Ignatius Press, 1996.

Snell, R. J. "Education and the Restoration of Moral Agency." *Public Discourse.* August 17, 2020.

Chapter 11: School Sports and Physical Education

Chesterton, G. K. *Collected Works, Vol. XXVII: The Illustrated London News 1905–1907.* San Francisco: Ignatius Press, 1986.

John Paul II. "Address to the Players, Trainers, and Directors of Real Madrid, the Champion Soccer Club of Europe." September 16, 2002.

———. "Jubilee of Sports People." October 29, 2000.

Chapter 12: Art

Consolmagno, Guy quoted in Sandra Sutton. "Seeing God in the Stars," *Midland Daily News.* August 12, 2003.

John Paul II. *Letter to Artists.* April 4, 1999.

McLuhan, Marshall. *Understanding Media: The Extensions of Man.* 1964.

Ratzinger, Joseph with Vitterio Messori. *The Ratzinger Report: An Exclusive Interview on the State of the Church.* San Francisco: Ignatius Press, 1985.

Tolkien, J. R. R. "Ainulindalë," in *The Silmarillion.* 1977.

———. "Leaf by Niggle." 1945.

———. "On Faerie Stories."

———. *The Lord of the Rings* trilogy.

About the Author

B rett Salkeld, Ph.D., is archdiocesan theologian for the Archdiocese of Regina in Canada. He earned his Ph.D. in systematic theology from Regis College at the Toronto School of Theology and has a bachelor's degree in education from the University of Regina, where he studied to become a social studies and math teacher. He has worked with graduate and undergraduate education students and with Catholic teachers in various professional-development settings. He lives in Regina, Saskatchewan, with his wife, Flannery, and their seven children.